# GOD HATES YOU

*The Experiment and Your Purpose Explained*

JEREMY LAVERGNE

**author**HOUSE®

*AuthorHouse™*
*1663 Liberty Drive*
*Bloomington, IN 47403*
*www.authorhouse.com*
*Phone: 833-262-8899*

*Published by AuthorHouse 07/27/2021*

*ISBN: 978-1-6655-3257-0 (sc)*
*ISBN: 978-1-6655-3255-6 (hc)*
*ISBN: 978-1-6655-3256-3 (e)*

*Library of Congress Control Number: 2021914837*

# CONTENTS

(This book is dedicated to the world)

Before you were born, God hated you, your children, and your children's children, and this moment in your life will prove whether he was right or wrong about having animosity towards you. God has been longing for you to know who he truly is and why he created this life for you to live—here on earth. Long before you first heard of God you were nothing; not even a thought or the size of a mustard seed; now the purpose of your body, mind, heart and soul is just consuming time and space.

This is a God who will 1-(have other gods), 2-(considers him or herself an idol), 3-(uses your name in vain), 4-(never honors you), 5-(never respects you), 6-(murders you), 7-(leaves you sad and broken), 8-(steals from you), 9-(lies against you), 10-(covets you), and as he participates in these aspects, forbids you to do so: can you say hypocrite; (KJV)-Exodus 20:2-17. Look inside your soul for the truth, it does exist.

This life is based on a matter of chance, the luck of the draw, and no one ever said that life was fair, not even him. I am so pleased that I do not have to exhaust myself with the foolishness and irrationality of this world any longer. I have been given me the real truth, and I no longer concede to worldly thoughts and motives. The aspiration of this presentation is for you to grow leaps and bounds, conform to greater elements in life, and leave the menial bearings behind-but will you? You can hate God and God can hate you, but if you obey the orders, you can cross into the gates of heaven. But will or won't you obey is the question. If you do not, then you will spend eternity in hades/hell. It is, literally, that plain and simple.

Letter from your author

# ALMIGHTY GOD'S MEMO TO HIS CREATION

<u>Vanity</u> means the pointless, meaningless actions of human activity throughout life without the involvement of God.

I, your creator, your true god named Yahweh, (YHWH)-referred to as the tetragrammaton, have always existed; for trillions, sextillion, decillion, maybe even for some centillion years, but I will never tell you my exact age, this is something you do not need to know. Many slaves have come before you and more will follow. What you do need to know is that I secretly hate and am jealous of you, my own creation; I am selfish and do not love myself, so there is no possible way that I could ever love you. Why would I create something that I could never love? The reason for this is that I became bored with life; I had no one to communicate with, I needed revelry and had a yearning to preside over you. I am the one that cannot be tamed, the one the witness cannot name, I have hate in my heart, and revenge in my brain.

Therefore, I created angels, demons, the planets, you, animals, insects, sun, moon, stars and the earth without asking for your opinion or needing your approval; already perceiving that you could never handle all that comes with life: knowing the hurt and pain you would go through, the horrible things you would experience, mental problems, disappointments and so much more. I am the boss and what I say goes, and I really do not care what you think. I am a cruel, unjust, jealous, unfair, arrogant, domineering, smug God. I led you to believe that I was loving, kind, and generous. I believed that by telling you I loved you, you would obey, but that did not work out either, as you still and will always do what you please.

I will never stop pestering, hassling, punishing, and sending trouble your way. I do this to you, because I am the liar, telling you that I will heal your sorrow, anguish, and affliction; but never do: instead, bringing more fires from my heavens upon you. I am the author of disaster, suffering, and strife, blaming it on my partner in crime, Satan, just read the books and they will tell you the truth. Your <u>reality</u> is your existence. From (KJV)-Isaiah 45:7; in the King James Version Bible, I say; "I form the light, and create darkness; I make peace, and I create evil; I the lord do all these things.", I, your creator, almighty God Yahweh do these things to you. From the (KJV)-the book of Proverbs 6:16-19 it says;" There are six things the lord hates, seven that are detestable to him: they are haughty eyes, a lying tongue, hands that shed innocent blood, a heart that devises wicked schemes, feet that are quick to rush into evil, a false witness who pours out lies, and a person who stirs up conflict in the community." These are the motives that I carry out; I am the hypocrite; as it is okay for me to sin, but not you. I did not know what I was doing when I created you; and it got out of control very quickly. I will never, ever apologize and admit my mistake to you because I am too prideful and boastful. Do you think it is easy being me, well yes; it is; as I will not stand for you disobeying me. I will send you to a place called hell in one swift second and be finished with your soul. You are but sand in the wind to me.

Do you honestly believe that if I truly loved you, I would allow you to live in this horrific and abhorrent life, day in and day out; then send you to hell for defying me? This should tell you that I do not love you, by sending you somewhere specifically designed for Satan and his demons. (KJV)-Luke 16:22-26 tells the story of a rich man in hell, saying; "The time came when the beggar died and the angels carried him to Abraham's side. The rich man also died and was buried. In hell, where (the rich man) was in torment, he looked up and saw Abraham far away, with Lazarus by his side. So he called to him, 'Father Abraham, have pity on me and send Lazarus to dip the tip of his finger in water and cool my tongue, because I am in agony in this fire."(QUR)-The Heifer 2:15 God says; "It is God who ridicules them, you and leaves them bewildered in their transgression."

(QUR)-Victory 48:5-6; "He will admit the believers, male and female, into Gardens beneath which rivers flow, to abide therein forever, and He will remit their sins. That, with God, is a great triumph. And He will punish the hypocrites, male and female, and the idolaters, male and female, those who harbor evil thoughts about God. They are surrounded by evil; and God is angry with them, and has cursed them, and has prepared for them Hell—a miserable destination."

Please read on, and you will discover all the reasons why I hate you immensely.

# DAY 1: STAGE 1

Evil arises not from a substance; but from the perversion of a will-(the creators will, not your will)-God has you believing that you are a bad person, a horrible human being, condemning you for living the life he gave you, the way you see fit. (KJV)-1 John ch 5: v 14 says; "And this is the confidence that we have toward him, that if we ask anything according to HIS will, he hears us." You believe that you are in control of your life: but you are not, the creator has jurisdiction over your circumstances and conditions. He does not care what the desires of YOUR will and heart are!

Heed my warning: do not love this life! God did not create you out of love and certainly not to be his friend; he created you so he could be your master-plain and simple. You were put in a position in which you cannot win. Would you believe me if I told you that everything in life were the opposite; well, you should? That good is evil and evil is good, that it is the ones who believe they are winners who are the true losers; and the losers who are the true winners. The ones who believe they are full are empty and the ones who are empty are full; the ones who are happy are sad and vice versa. (KJV)-1 Peter ch 2: v 16 says; "Live as free people, but do not use your freedom as a cover-up for evil; live as God's slaves." (KJV)-Hosea ch 4: v 6 says; "My people are destroyed for lack of knowledge; because you have rejected knowledge, I also reject you as my priests; because you have ignored the law of your God, I also will ignore your children."

Stress on a daily basis, it should not have to be this way?

1

A day, week, month, year of your life, it is 5:00 pm where you live, and you are driving the speed limit anticipating your arrival home where you can catch your breath from the day. However, before you can realize this, you look up in your rear view mirror and see a young person giving you the middle finger, blowing their horn at you, probably upset because you are travelling the legal limit required on your path and you are not speeding. Chances are they are in a rush to get to a destination that they have seen many times over, nothing new. You do not respond, you just put your eyes back on the road to concentrate on not getting in an accident. You drive a few more miles down the freeway, and then suddenly, someone else cuts in front of you, trying to beat traffic and get ahead of you, leaving a very narrow space to spare. You blow your horn at them, and this person gives you two middle fingers, taking their hands off the wheel, endangering more lives in the process. You can see them cursing you in their vehicle. You had to slam on your breaks to avoid this calamity, and say to yourself, let it go, move on, this world is crazy and it is what it is; you have to cope with it. That person will never stress about this incident, so I suggest you do the same.

After this aggravating ride home, you finally arrive home and as soon as you take a step into the front door, your children beg for attention. They are of young ages, so it is important to them. You play games with them for a moment, asking how their day at school was. Then your wife comes in to meet you in the hallway and you have a small disagreement with her right before dinner, concerning the overdue mortgage payment and other bills, and it puts a strain on the atmosphere at the dinner table. You both put on a good face to show that everything is fine, knowing that it is not. Therefore, you eat your dinner trying to keep the peace for your children's sake. Later, lying in bed, you decide to watch some news before trying to fall asleep. All you hear about is chaos; killing's, lawsuits, civil unrest, floods, etc. You think to yourself, is there anything good in the world to report on anymore. Thus, you turn the television off and try to get some rest.

Let us back up a bit to earlier that day; where you just finished working a nine-hour shift at the office filled with putting out one issue after another; having to deal with demanding questions and requests in your field of employment from clients and bosses. And having to do double your normal work because you ask co-workers to help out some, but they do not know how to perform their tasks correctly, or is it just plain laziness. All the while, working in a field that you did not go to college for, because it offered a better salary, somehow getting your foot in the door and learning the business from the bottom up. Making matters worse, your mother is sick and getting worse by the day. You also received a bill from the tax department of your country within the last week stating that you owe on this year's return. You happened to get it before your wife did, so you hide it from her, because you are not ready to talk about this just yet. You try to control the stress because you do not want it to show to your family. But you wonder why? Why does it have to be this way? Why can't I have a simple life, why does it have to be filled with one troublesome affair after the next? You are on a fixed salary, so you cannot make overtime to cover the extra expenses.

You wonder how can you make it work and secondly, just when you are saving some money, you are going to have to dip into savings and will set you back. Then you start worrying about all sorts of items, like how to pay for the children's college funds if they cannot get a scholarship, the new car that is needed, house repairs, the electricity bill that keeps getting higher every quarter, etc. etc. etc. When will it ever stop, when will it ever end? You have had enough of this struggle; enough of whatever this life is that we live. How can I get ahead in life, have some freedom and peace, both emotionally and financially? In addition, this is just you, your life, your problems, your hardships. Well my friend, there is a reason our lives are this way, and you will not be happy when you learn the real truth. p.s.

To top off your Monday, you must wake up the next morning, and do it all over again! You are similar to a frog, going about his daily routine, living life, nature, his body and suddenly a snake devours him for lunch, the frog ceasing to exist anymore. One quick note, it should be called the d.s.a-the divided states of America and not the usa because no state or person has been doing the same throughout the history of this country.

## **The Truth**

I am not on the side of God Yahweh-the supposedly good, loving god and father of Jesus Christ or God Satan-the hateful god and father of the antichrist or the mortal God-you, the confused creation walking the earth: my only motive is that you comprehend the complete truth. Yahweh never lied to you; he told you exactly what would happen to you from living in this world through the bible. But you never expected that it would be this bad, this hard, right; the hurt, pain, suffering, crying, confusion, boredom and aches, but reality is that it is this bad and this God Yahweh-creator is not who you think he is. (QUR)-The Spreaders 51:56 god says; "I did not create the angels, demons, jinn and the humans except to worship Me."

You are so busy with living your vanity filled life that you cannot see what goes on behind the scenes. But the world is not what it seems to be, or is it: the nightmare that is your life IS what it is supposed to be because your creator is the nightmare! You will not get any closer to God than where you are right now. (KJV)-Lamentations 3:37-38; "Who is he that can speak, and it happens, when the lord command it not? Out of the mouth of the most high proceeds both evil and good?" It is he, the good god Yahweh-father of Jesus Christ that proclaims evil and good, carries it out his devices through God Satan, the instrument and Satan carries it further through you, the pawn. I list this next verse again because it is so crucial in your understanding of how and why your loving, creating god Yahweh is the true evil one; all the while blaming evil on Satan.

Your reality is your existence. From (KJV)-Isaiah 45:7; in the King James Version Bible, saying; "I form the light, and create darkness; I make peace, and I create evil; I the lord do all these things." I, your creator, almighty God Yahweh do these things to you. I need you to concentrate on him proclaiming that he is responsible for evil, how could you have missed this? I, your author of this book, am not a prophet, spirit, seer, or prognosticator; I am a real and honest person that goes through this difficult life just as you do; but sees the truth for what it is, using only true and actual verses given to us by Yahweh; showing you what you already know, the kind of God you truly have: nor do I desire the responsibility of being a prophet. (KJV)-1 John 4:1; "Beloved, do not believe every spirit, but test the spirits to see whether they are from God, for many false prophets have gone out into the world." What does God want from you when He cannot follow his own rules.

## **Let's be Honest**

This God Yahweh, your creator; wants to fight you, a human being; how does this make any sense at all? If you are in the 60%-70% of the world that is currently employed; this is your life of daily work. However, if you fit into the 30%-40% category that is unemployed, well, you have these affairs plus many, many more. The good, loving almighty God Yahweh tells us that he is the solution, but I am here to ask; have you ever thought or believed that he is the cause, the topic, and the root of all our problems? This entity has everyone fooled thinking he is the greatest thing in the universe, but in your reality, he is the source and main reason; we as human beings, live a tumultuous and hard life from its inception. Do you feel unsatisfied with life, the things you have or have not accomplished; loneliness even though you are married, have friends, and even wealth, still wanting more; no direction for your life, well, there is a reason for that. You have read self-help, spiritual books, seen psychologists and life coaches, but none have answered the provocative questions you desire. If you can manage the patience needed to get through these 30 stages, you will have the meaning and understanding of life. To answer this question, of course you are always unhappy and fatigued. In the Bible; God is responsible for over 250 billion deaths or more, while Satan is responsible for only 10, all of which God Yahweh commanded him to do.

In case you never knew, it did not have to be this way. Life did not have to be this hard and frustrating. Why would someone or something do this to us? Why would they put us through all this desolation, hunger, sadness, loneliness, stress, strife, burden, worry, etc., of this life? From the (KJV)-the book of Matthew 10:34-39; "Do not suppose that I have come to bring peace to the earth. I did not come to bring peace, but a sword. For I have come to turn a man against his father, a daughter against her mother, a daughter-in-law against her mother-in-law, a man's enemies will be the members of his own household. Anyone who loves their father or mother more than me is not worthy of me; anyone who loves their son or daughter more than me is not worthy of me. Whoever does not take up their cross and follow me is not worthy of me. Whoever finds their life will lose it, and whoever loses their life for my sake will find it." Those are the words that came from the mouth of your savior 'Jesus Christ'; does this sound like a loving, caring, gentle person/entity? The almighty God Yahweh and Jesus Christ claim to be the good and nice entities but make no mistake about it; these are broken, disturbed, depressing spirits.

My friend, guess what, your loving almighty God Yahweh purposely designed life this way, just for you. In addition, this is the entity you worship and praise for a couple hours on Sunday. You send up prayers that never draw an answer; throwing your hands up in the air asking for help, with no alleviation, wondering why you never hear from your God. Well, God made exactly what he wanted, and how he wanted it; when he created this world and everything in the matrix. He should practice what he preaches, with the old saying, 'be careful what you wish for'.

The God that you know as your creator is a cruel, hateful, evil, unjust, narcissistic, domineering tyrant. He wanted chaos; he got it, he wanted hate; he got it, he wanted killing; he got it, he wanted cruelty; he got it all between humanity. Not only in our age of living, but from the birth of its commencement. Between the first set of brothers to ever live, God positioned them against one another, and eventually the oldest killed the younger brother out of jealously; Cain killing Abel. What were they doing: trying to please a God that can never be satisfied and gratified.

I will be using scriptures from the King James Version Bible-(KJV), the Quran-(QUR), the 41 books that were removed from the (KJV) called the apocrypha and Pseudepigrapha books, hidden texts, dead sea scrolls, and your reality, so no one can tell me I do not know what I am saying, because I do. These two books: the (KJV) and (QUR) essentially tell the exact story, scenarios, ideas, with the same people involved; just worded differently. I firmly believe that the state of religion placed the two books against one another to start wars, make political statements, access financial gain, and say that my God is bigger and better than yours: but in reality, they are the same God. I believe both books originated in the same location but took a separate path in the world, Quran going to eastern southern Europe, and King James Version going to western northern Europe, and then spread throughout the world as we know of today. I use both to prove to you that we are discussing the same God or Gods and we have no reason to fight and kill over this any longer as a human race. These Gods are playing you and have turned you against one another: it is time that you realize this!

## My Reason

(QUR)-The Table 5:18; "the jews and Christians say, "We are the children of god, and his beloved. Say, Why then does he punish you for your sins? In fact, you are humans from among those he created. He forgives whom he wills, and he punishes whom he wills. To god belongs the heavens and the earth and what lies between them, and to him is the return."

What I do not cover in this presentation, I have listed many terrific authors that cover many valuable subjects that you may be interested in after reading this. I give a list of authors in stage thirty-two. What I am presenting to you, is the simple and plain fact; that the almighty God hates you. This is not a novel; it is a fact on facts presentation. Quoted from the (KJV)-in 1 Corinthians 4:6; "Do not go beyond what is written in the book", I will not, only using scripture to show you what kind of almighty God and creator we are dealing with. Let us open up the door right away with each other! I neither love nor hate the Gods, but wow, this world sucks. The God that supposedly created us never intended to make this a happy, pleasant, merry, and delightful world for us to live in. It is so evident, that it is laughable to believe that God could ever love us and wanted us to be happy here. I wrote this for three reasons, and will catch a lot of backlash over it, but you must know the truth, and I can take any and all reactions you have to it. People are always afraid of matters that they do not understand; and my friends, you never understood what this Creator is really like.

#1:  I started writing as a way to release my revelations: get things off my chest;

#2:  To say what people have always felt and speculated; but too afraid to admit;

#3:  To tell you the truth, and if it can help you, then you are welcome; if not, well;

## The biggest lie ever told?

The biggest lie ever told in the history of the world, is that the almighty, creator God Yahweh loves you. The fact is, he does not love you. It is hard to except, but you are one of trillions of people who have ever lived and walked on this planet that we call earth since its dawn. What makes you more special from the person standing next to you; I know you believe you are better than the next but you are not; not a single thing. I realize that you want to believe you are the most important person in the cosmos, but this is simply incorrect.

Every man and woman has the same body part. (KJV)-Ecclesiastes 6:3; "A man may father a hundred children and live many years. No matter how long he lives, if he is not satisfied by good things and does not even have a proper burial, I say that a stillborn child is better off than he." Whether you were a developing baby that died in the womb and never received a chance at life; to dying in a car accident at 40; to actually living your life out to being 100 years old and passing away, your life never mattered as all this was designed by chance. It does not matter to him if you are a CEO of a fortune 500 company, or a person living on a street corner that fell on hard times and could not dig themselves out of the hole. You cannot escape and look beyond the evidence of how he treats you and fellow human beings.

God views our world in quantity, not quality. Your outlook on ants is similar to how God sees you. and you are stuck on this ant pile called earth. You are not more special and sophisticated than the people you cross paths with during the course of your life! Just like you can destroy a million ants at one time and not give a care in the world about them, is the same thing being done to you by God, you just never realized it before. He has allowed so many

Do you feel like this more often than not?

horrific events to happen to humanity that was unnecessary. For what reason; because it fits into his 'ultimate, sovereign, glorious plan'.

The first section of the books removed is called the 'Books of Apocrypha', and contains nineteen books. Apocrypha's meaning is described as "biblical writings excluded because they were not a forming part of the accepted canon of Scripture according to religious leaders". Adding to this, the apocrypha books were written between the old and new testament, the time when Jesus walked on the earth. With all the people that lived during Jesus's time on earth, only a very small percentage believed in what he had to say, so leaders try and have tried anything and everything to discredit him. Therefore, it is plain to see why the apocrypha books where eliminated, and hidden, but it does not take away the fact that they were written and are accurate.

The second section not included, is the 'Books of Pseudepigrapha', and contains twenty-one books. Pseudepigrapha comes from the Greek word meaning 'false writings'. The meaning of Pseudepigrapha sounds somewhat dubious, but I told you the real meaning of these two books because I have nothing to hide, but certain people do. People will always try to discredit something if it hits to close to home. In addition, if you do not know by now, I hope you will by reading through this presentation, that there are many people who hate their own life and want to make others' lives as miserable as theirs. So yes, they have given the meaning of false writings to Pseudepigrapha, because leaders

Is this worth it?

in any level of religion, business, education, entertainment, cults, military and government have taken extreme measures to conceal these messages from you, and to deceive you into believing they were not established. Why does this sound all too familiar? Well, because these types of people figured they could tell you what they wanted you to know, and leave out the rest: for the simple matter of controlling you. These messages have come from God himself, but because people have always wanted to control and conquer the world, they kept you in the dark. Go ahead; be my guest, throughout the history of the world, there has always been someone in every generation trying to rule the world. Therefore, between God and the men and women that he has allowed to run the world, you live in a world of bondage; from your birth to your death. Loving almighty God Yahweh does not want to love you, he wants you to fear him coming from (KJV)- Psalm 90:11; "Who knows the power of your anger? For your wrath is as great as the fear that is due you."

## <u>My purpose to you</u>

B.S.: this is not a piece of scripture; it is a poem called 'footprints in the sand'. This was written by man, for the sole purpose of profit. The poem has a picture showing one set of footprints in the sand claiming that god is the one carrying you when times are rough. No my friends, god has left you alone, and always has-if your will does not align with his will, that set of footprints is you walking all by yourself. From the (QUR)-Family of Imran 3:4-5; "A foretime, as guidance for mankind; and He sent down the Criterion. Those who have rejected God's signs will have a severe punishment. God is mighty, able to take revenge. Nothing is hidden from God, on earth or in the heaven."

My question to you is; what did we ever do to God, for him to seek revenge on us, a denomination of people who do not possess the means and capabilities to defend ourselves against him? I am not denying his existence. There is undeniable evidence that someone or something put us here on this planet. I just know that the God that created you does not love, as his actions have proven otherwise. We were lied to about our existence and purpose. The world that you and I live in; is and always will be, just a game to this individual, and you were created as an experiment, not out of love. All this really is, when you walk out your front door every day, is a coherent creation assembled as advertised, based off the saying; 'let the chips fall where they may'. Your almighty God does not care who you are, whether you are rich or poor, beautiful or ugly, tall or short, smart or dumb, happy or sad: none of this matters to him.

For example, from a global standpoint, suppose you happened to be born in Nigeria, a barren and heavily unemployed, poor country; while someone else was born in the usa, apparently full of opportunity and life, is this a fair way to start your beginnings? No, it is not. One person has the world and opportunity at their fingertips; while the other strives only to obtain food and water for the day, so they will not starve to death. Or on a personal level, what about the young lady that walks around on a daily basis, with internal scars, wondering why God gave her an ugly appearance, and she is not as beautiful as other women? Missing opportunities and down on herself because she could not have the same luck of the draw and be appealing and sexy as other women. Nevertheless, there is a gorgeous woman on the other side of this scenario, reaping the earthly rewards of being beautiful. Is this fair, I will let you be the judge.

Please wake up humanity, we were lied to and fooled. I challenge you to take a step back from this world, stop watching the foolishness and stupidity that is television, stop playing video games for a day, stop texting worthless information on your phones, stop believing what someone else tells you to believe, and look inside your soul, and be honest with yourself about what this life really is. I am not here to have scientific discussions and arguments, giving you pages and pages of mind-numbing worthless information; by calculating the shape of the world, who said what and didn't say what between the 1,100-1,800 century, and am not trying to convert you from the current religion you follow, or prove why there is something instead of nothing, etc. From the (QUR)-The Livestock 6:6 angels saying; "Have you not considered how many generations we destroyed before you? We had established them on earth more firmly than we established you, and we sent the clouds pouring down abundant rain on them, and we made rivers flow beneath them. But we destroyed them for their sins, and established other civilizations after them." Evil befalls on those who love God and those who do not; so what is the difference? So if you are ready to start this journey, let us begin. In the midst of life; we are in death. (QUR)-The Table 5:33; "The punishment for those who fight God and His messenger, and strive to spread corruption on earth, is that they be killed, or crucified, or have their hands and feet cut off on opposite sides, or be banished from the land. That is to disgrace them in this life; and in the Hereafter they will have a terrible punishment." I am not fighting God Yahweh, only telling you the truth. He never wanted you to know the truth. Yahweh is the true tyrant who wants to cut your hands and feet off for disobeying his commandments. This God Yahweh helps who he wants and does not for those he cared nothing for. I do not consider myself a prophet, teacher, psychic, monk, or scholar, just a man who sees this world for what it really is and his reality. You are more with less and less with more! This is a god who plants wonderful items in front of you and tells you; no, you cannot have it! If you ask for things in your will, it will not happen. If you ask for things in his will, it still may not happen. For thousands, maybe even millions of years, people have always tried to find the good in bad situations, but you cannot find good when he is a bad god. I did not, you did not, no one asked for this world and the way it is.

Let's move on.

# DAY 2: STAGE 2

All God really is; is d.o.g spelled backwards.

Who are these three entities? God controls you out of fear; not love. Yahweh-the loving god, made a deal with Satan-the hateful god, for your soul: and you, most of the world's population would claim to know and interpret what scripture speaks of; then when you start getting into the logistics of it, they do not know a single thing, or get it all wrong. You must know whom you are dealing with and you do not. Based off what the universe has been taught to believe; religious followers and even the non-religious world would agree that there is a good God and an evil God. And that one God always existed; and the other was created. I do believe this to be true-that all others were created-as there are verses saying that Lucifer-God Satan was created, angels and demons. But the second god was created for the sole purpose of being evil and they play the constant game of good and evil between your lives. The creating god knew all along that the other would turn evil and still let it happen. Satan and Jesus Christ are brothers. Can you comprehend for one second that maybe you were conned; and that there were two gods, even many gods instead of one. That one took the blame for the other, as part of their plan, a long, long time ago, one decided to be good, and the other evil, and they made a contract for your soul. This is not too hard to believe, since; who has seen either one face to face, as they conceal themselves from us and let us go about living our daily lives.

For the sake of our understanding throughout the rest of this book; let us call one God = 'the good God; Yahweh', the other God = 'the evil God; Satan', and the third God = 'the mortal God; you'. There will always be resistance in the world, no matter what you are involved in, two opposing forces pulling against each other, and it began with these two at the top of the food chain. The two Gods are allegedly against each other, good against evil, but still take upon a business partnership between one another for your soul. We are caught in the middle of a trap, which you can call the matrix; being played between these two entities. Each partner is personally liable for all debts incurred by the business. The partners report their share of profits or losses on their individual tax returns, as part of their regular income. A partnership is described as:

> ➤ A type of business organization in which two or more individuals' pull money, skills, and other resources, and share profit and losses in accordance with terms of the partnership agreement. Participants in an enterprise agree to share the associated risks and rewards proportionately.

To understand anything in life, you must start from the very, very beginning. As humans, we always look for the easy way out. You must remove yourself from continuing this sort of behavior. I will explain many misconceptions throughout this book, but let me introduce one important overlooked misinterpretation to begin. We are inaccurately two thousand years after the death of Jesus Christ and still cannot get our creator's names correct. Elohim is said to mean 'many Gods', so when you speak of a God, you have to be careful of who you are directing your words to....... because in (KJV)-Genesis 1:26; "Let us make man in OUR image, in OUR likeness, and let them rule over the fish of the sea and the birds of the air, over the livestock, over the earth, and over all the creatures that move along the ground." Right here in this verse, it is telling you there are many Gods. If there were one God, he would have said 'in MY image', but instead, they said 'in OUR image'.

There is one clear name that the good God wants to be called, and one that the evil God is called, but we do not call them by their names. Reason for this is that anything can be a God; your money, car, clothes, hair, jewelry, etc. can be a particular individuals God. I want to clarify which Gods we are talking about in this chapter, as I am discussing the two Gods that created us and put us here on this worthless planet called earth. I do hope that anyone reading this would agree; that we were created, and that we did not come from monkeys or gorillas, and that the belief in the big bang theory and evolution is; well, a ridiculous concept. These two foolish ideas were developed and designed by mankind to stray the general public/masses from the truth. You were designed by a being, a creator, as you are too resourceful, intelligent, and canny to believe otherwise. I say to you, as a people and a society, it is time that we started acting as such; rational and wise beings.

A cult is defined as a system of religious veneration and devotion directed towards a particular figure or object. By my understanding, the Gods are not an object, they are spiritual beings. Cults in smaller communities across the world have always received a bad name, but if you are in the Catholic, Christian, Baptist, Islam, Hinduism, Mormon, Agnosticism, New-Age-Scientology, Buddhism, Protestant, Atheism, Anglicanism, Sikhism, Seventh-Day Adventists, Latter Day Saints, or Judaism church, etc, etc, etc, you are in a cult. You all claim to be better than the next when your own soul is not saved. We were directed to worship one God; so why

> God Yahweh: man created in his image

do you have over 7,500-10,000 different registered religions at any given time across our globe? These things do not make sense!

## Discussing: the good God Yahweh

This God clearly states that he wants to be called: "YAHWEH-I am that I am", or "I am" as in (KJV)-Exodus 3:14, when god said to Moses; "I am who I am", or YAHWEH in deep biblical translation, or "He Brings into Existence Whatever Exists." This is what you are to say to the Israelites: "I AM' has sent me to you." This is the name of the so-called good God; the name he gave to Moses when instructing him to lead the Israelites out of slavery from the Egyptians. I will call the supposedly good god 'Yahweh': this name is made up of 4 Hebrew consonants (YHWH) called the tetragrammaton. Ancient Hebrew was written using only consonants-no vowels. So Yahweh was written YHWH. Around the first century AD it became common for Jews to avoid speaking God's name, Yahweh, for fear of doing so too casually and thus breaking the second commandment, (KJV)-Exodus 20:7; "You shall not take the name of the Lord your God in vain,". The name Yahweh comes from a Hebrew word meaning "to be" or "to exist." Because He is self-existent, Yahweh is the source of life for everything and everyone else. The Bible is the story of God and the salvation He offers; but at what costs, you did nothing wrong?

In the third century, people ceased to use this name for two reasons. One, they preferred to use the name Elohim as a universal sovereignty above all other Gods (they did not want to contact him directly); and two, the name was regarded as being so sacred, (that they did not feel comfortable using it out loud); but it is still the correct alias. Jesus Christ's real name is Yahushua, a branch of Yahweh; but I will call him Jesus as this is what you are conformed to. If this is the supposedly God of love, care, and concern; it simply does not make any sense that he would enslave his own creation, but this is exactly what he has done, and still does to you in this modern day. I definitely would not enslave someone that I loved, would you? This God is confusing, unstable and posing as a loving God, but is really a bully, oppressor, and slave master.

Created in the image of God means that you have a heart to love or hate, a mind to make decisions, and a body to operate in. According to scripture, this good God Yahweh has always existed and created the other one. This God is so angry that man and woman chose and continue to choose the option of sin instead of obeying his laws from the Garden of Eden. How can you trust someone that never gave you all the information firsthand? You cannot! But then he wants to punish and abuse people for disobeying his laws and living their life as they desire and see fit. This good

God has a son named Jesus Christ, and the holy spirit: as all three together are called the "The Holy Trinity".

This God Yahweh resigns in a place called heaven, but is a jealous, spiteful, and dangerous entity. (KJV)-Exodus 34:14, "Do not worship any other god, for the Lord, whose name is Jealous, is a jealous God." Hypocrites pray to this God, people who claim to be good; but acting upon dirty, unethical business and personal motives in the dark, hoping he will forgive them one day. This God claims to be of love, righteousness, forgiving, and patient; but will quickly turn his back on you, and send you to hell or hades (same place) for your unforgiven sins. Men and women of the clergy, priesthood, pastor hood, all know who this real God is, but they can never tell you, because they would never receive your tithes and offerings anymore. Religion needs these substances to survive, playing the tunes of a good and loving God; lying to you all the while. How do you even know that you are worshipping the correct God, when you do not refer to him by the appropriate name or term? You were made exactly like you were supposed to be made. When you partake in pleasurable events, you are happy and God is not. When you partake in un-pleasurable events, you are sad and God is happy. (QUR)-Kneeling 45:23; "Have you considered him who has taken his desire for his god? God has knowingly led him astray, and has sealed his hearing and his heart, and has placed a veil over his vision. Who will guide him after god? Will you not reflect?" Yahweh is God's personal name. The bible, and specifically the Book of Exodus, presents Yahweh as the god of the Israelites; there are many passages which make it very clear that this deity was also worshipped by other peoples in Canaan, Edomites, Kenites, Moabites, and Midianites all worshipped Yahweh to one degree or another. The most high's name is EL.

God Yahweh is your Elohim god of good and death.

# <u>Wake Up</u>

This subject has been weighing on my soul for a very long time, and I had to let the world be aware of the truth, for generations and generations long after I have taken my last breath. I had to tell the actuality about this creation called humans, earth, the invisible world of angels and demons, and everything involved between. We were misled, and our lives never mattered to the good God or the evil God. As human beings, when we take something serious in our lives, we do not make deals over our outcome: well, actually we do. Jesus said that your soul is worth more than the rest of the world put together, but a small percentage of you will reach the promised land. Is it this impossible for us to grasp what is meant by "the whole world." Jesus implied that if one soul can make it to heaven, it is worth more than the entire world. This is how your God Yahweh truly feels about you; saying that he does not care about all the souls that go to hell; if you refuse to believe in the person that is Jesus Christ, just that one soul that believes, reaches heaven. The evil God and his son, sit back and wait, as they know that people will not believe in a savior, especially when you cannot physically see him. With over 10,000 different religions/cults in the world, it seems to me like we cannot make up our minds as well, on who you prefer to worship.

# <u>**Discussing: the evil God Satan**</u>

This God has many names as well; Lucifer, the devil, but Satan is adopted. I will call the evil God 'Satan'. God Satan has a region called hell designed to torment you for every second of a second that you are in the fiery pits; teasing you with your favorite and appealing sins that were committed on earth. We should all know the history by now; depending on whether you were a good person or a bad person, will determine your eternal resting place. This God: 'the dragon or anti-god' has a son as well, named 'the beast or anti-christ', and 'the false prophet or anti-spirit'. They are called "The Satanic Trinity". At least we know what type of personality this one keeps. He hates us, that is a given fact, all day and every day; as (KJV)-John 10:10; "The thief cometh not, but that he may steal, and kill, and destroy."

According to scripture, he is very powerful entity as well. If the good God Yahweh was in total control of the universe, would it make sense that he would allow the amount of evil we experience in this physical

world from the evil God Satan, allowing Satan to run around and do what he pleases. Our world is a playground for them, and it would seem like we should be worth more than what the good God is fighting for, but apparently; we are not. If Satan was menial; he would not have this much control over the earth, the air, natural power, and a place called hell to rule in. He has an army of demons that are dangerous and hateful as him towards us. He is accused of bringing sin into the world, but sin always existed, as virtue has. He is the one that gets the blame for evil; but make no mistake about it, the good God is just as harmful to you.

This is the statue of the Baphomet; the representation of the God Satan. You have maybe seen this before but didn't know what it was. It has been known to travel, and in some places, it has been seen is in front of the Vatican, the capital of the United States, Hollywood, the British Parliament, Africa. It represents the Satanic Temple.

This evil God is predictable and balanced, which makes the good God even more deadly; as God Yahweh is ambiguous and insecure. God Satan is stable and only wants one thing, to be considered the greatest being to ever live. He will stop at nothing for his worship and praise. The bible never calls him an angel fallen from heaven. The word "Satan" does not occur in the (KJV) book of Genesis, which mentions only a talking serpent; which is actually him, with the ability to take shape, form, and size of anything. But his name does occur in (QUR)-The Heifer 2:34; "And we said to the angels, "Bow down to Adam." They bowed down, except for Satan. He refused, was arrogant, and was one of the disbelievers." He was above the angels and my conclusion is that he is equal to the power of God Yahweh. I believed God Yahweh bowed down to Adam, the first man to exist, but God Satan refused to give Adam glory. Lucifer is Satan's personal name. God Satan is your Elohim God of evil.

## Discussing the mortal God, You

The third God is you. I have learned by discussing and reading their books; that priests, pastors, and men of the clergy etc., all say that we are not Gods. I am here to tell you, that they are complete fools. They claim to know the scriptures, but miss many critical points. The minute that Adam ate the apple from the tree, you became a God. I am sorry ladies, I did not make the rules; but Eve could have eaten as many apples as she wanted, God put the power in the man. It seems that science and religion are two complementary aspects of our cognitive, social, and historical lives. To prove to you that you are a God, Jesus Christ even called you a God, in (KJV)-John 10:34; "Is it not written in your law, 'I said', you are gods!" If you were not a God, you wouldn't have been given the chance to make decisions for yourself, such as in the belief that we have free will.

You are in control of your own body and mind, for the moment; you decide where you go in life, what you consume, what career you want to have, what you say, who you love, so yes, you are a god, but you are a limited God, by time and space. We all know that we are born and then will pass away: that is a given, a promise if you will. The man God has always intended to do his own thing; to never be controlled, and make his or her own decisions and

Are you and your significant other reading two different books?

agendas. This has always been the problem between the three Gods; as each is playing tug a war with one another and will be the case for the duration of the experiment.

- <u>Knowledge</u> = facts, information, and skills acquired by a person through experience or education; the theoretical or practical understanding of a subject.
- <u>Wisdom</u> = the soundness of an action or decision with regard to the application of experience, knowledge, and good judgment.

We are simple creatures, no matter which way you want to look at it; our knowledge and wisdom here on earth is not our struggle, it is with eternity. We do not want to be told what to do, to be judged, and where we will spend eternity; but are currently setting the table for our spot on our own accords, based off personal decisions and actions. We want to be in control of ourselves in every sense of the word, and we are not. It scares us to death to have a decision made for us, and be in a position that is opposite of supervising. We have great and wonderful people here on earth; but also have despicable and hateful ones. The good God Yahweh even tells us that we are not promised heaven; but you are guaranteed hell. This is what makes our world, the fight between a supposedly good, and evil God, all the more difficult. We cannot win playing this game, and in our world, the good God is mad that the world follows the way of the evil God, and he holds it against us. I know you have to do what you are going to do to survive, but what you are doing, it is not going to last, no matter how big you think you get in the eyes of the world, it means nothing, it will always turn out bad. Your creators are not who you think they are. Your life; is just a business deal, a risky venture. What God ultimately wants if for you to suffer, but you do not desire this: it is a never ending cycle of tug of war. (QUR)-The Unleashed 77:7; "Surely what you are promised will happen." You can protect yourself against evil when you see it coming, but cannot protect yourself against good turning bad; you cannot see when it turns until it is too late.

I have seen a person go a whole lifetime and not know who God is: but I will tell you.

# DAY 3: STAGE 3

The Gods set you up to fail from the very beginning.

You will never look at life the same way after reading this presentation: and if I told you everything, I mean everything; you would not want anything to do with this God Yahweh or God Satan, so I am keeping it short and brief. I am limited by time, space, words, and pages. (QUR)-The Most High 87:5; "Except what God wills, he knows what is declared, and what is hidden."(QUR)-Kneeling 45:16; 'We gave the children of Israel the book, and wisdom, and prophecy; and we provided them with the good things; and we gave them advantage over all other people." The experiment, called the 'Garden of Eden' and 'your life', continues for man and woman in our day and age. There were two specific trees in the Garden of Eden, one called the "tree of life" and the other, "the tree of knowledge of good and evil". This was first mentioned in (KJV)-the book of Genesis, 2:9. Citizens of the world, you were led to believe that you were deceived by the evil God Satan, but this is a lie. Your creator cheated you. According to scripture, Yahweh claims that Satan was the one who deceived the whole world in (KJV)-Revelation, 12:9; "And the great dragon was thrown down, that ancient serpent, who is called the devil and Satan, the deceiver of the whole world—he was thrown down to the earth, and his angels were thrown down with him." It was both of them.

(KJV)-Genesis 2:8-14 is saying where the garden is located in what is now current Iraq; "The Lord God planted a garden eastward in Eden. . . . Now a river went out of Eden to water the garden, and from there it parted and became four riverheads. The name of the first is Pishon, to the south. . . . The name of the second river is Gihon, to the north. . . . The name of the third river is Tigris, to the east. . . . The fourth river is the Euphrates, to the west." One major topic I want to discuss before we get to far down the road: is how this good and loving God Yahweh-father of Jesus Christ thinks of you. He degrades this creation; he puts you, me, humanity down like a bully. Whether you are a man, woman, young adult, or child at the time of this reading, he demeans your status as a human being; you are never good enough. Mankind should have been made perfect but we were not. Continuing, this good and loving God Yahweh has the utmost class and style to create you as an imperfect being and criticizes you for sinning. He is constantly looking down at you in disgrace; knowing you cannot obey commandments and follow instructions, repeatedly reprimanding you for mistakes and wrong choices. What is the point in having this creation if all you are going to do is pass blame? Maybe it is time God Yahweh looks at himself in the mirror, it is not we who are wrong, it is you, God Yahweh! (KVJ)-Isaiah 64:6; "All of us have become like one who is unclean, and all our righteous acts are like filthy rags; we all shrivel up like a leaf, and like the wind our sins sweep us away." This is what you good God Yahweh thinks of you: no respect, no love, no concern!

Moving on, the truth of the matter is that the good God Yahweh is the one who betrayed the whole world, and it is he; who plays with your life and toys with your emotions. This happens in the very beginning of creation. If Adam, the first man, had eaten from "the tree of life"; all this struggle, hurt, hunger, and pain in the world that we experience on a daily basis would have been avoided. If Adam would have eaten from "the tree of life", man and woman would have been converted to and having powers greater than the angels have. He did not want this to happen though.

See, the good God only told Adam and Eve, the only two living human beings in the Garden of Eden, not to eat from one particular tree, and that tree was the 'tree of knowledge of good and evil'. He never mentioned anything about eating from the 'tree of life'. The tree of life would have made them live forever. He became greedy, he was not satisfied with only two souls, he wanted more, and more, until now we have over 8 billion souls living at one time on this planet. He definitely made sure he told them what could happen by eating from the 'tree of knowledge of good and evil, but never told them the repercussions of eating from the 'tree of life'. Why would he conceal such powerful information about the 'tree of life'? He could have told the two human beings the truth. Right then and there, humanities fate was sealed, when God Yahweh held an all to informative fact from Adam and Eve, which could have led to a different world than what we are living in today. The case being: eat from 'the tree of life' and we would receive life, but from 'the tree of knowledge of good and evil', we would receive death. As death is the type of life we have been living in ever since; a life of annihilation. The good God Yahweh does not want a good path of life for you, how is this not evident to you.

As a person, you want to be informed with as much information as possible about a situation so you can make the best levelheaded decision presented to you, without anything left out. That obvious answer is yes, but the God that claims to love us, withheld a core piece of data leading to the world, as we know it. God did not want us to be above the angels, because if he did, we would not have gone through this disaster of a life toiling, with daily physical exertions and pains. Anyone that claims that this life is good; is insane. Yes, I said it. This God Yahweh claims to be "The Great Almighty", and "The Great I Am", but this is the best that he came up with? A world filled with loneliness, heartache, killing, etc. The world you see today. So God purposely led us down the path of "the tree of knowledge of good and evil".

## **The Confrontation**

The two Gods confronted each other, and one said that he could be a better leader than the other. The challenge was accepted, and the rest is history; really, everything that came before us is history. This is crucial in understanding Yahweh's so called love, or lack of love, for you. Because at this point, Satan 'tempted' humanity in the initial stages of the experiment, and thousands of years later, is still doing the same. Yahweh does not care about your soul; and neither does Satan.

A key verse comes from (KJV)-John 8:44 which Jesus says; "You belong to your father, the devil, and you want to carry out your father's desires. He was a murderer from the beginning, not holding to the truth, for there is no truth in him. When he lies, he speaks his native language, for he is a liar and the father of lies. Yet because I tell you the truth, you do not believe me. Can any of you prove me guilty of sin? If I am telling the truth, why don't you believe me? He who belongs to God hears what God says. The reason you do not hear is that you do not belong to God." Why would such a verse be confirmed in the Bible and Quran? This verse is telling you, that you do not belong to God Yahweh, and that you are a child of God Satan; not God Yahweh as you were led to believe. Could he be the creator? This is why I tell you that both possibly created us. The bible came from the tongue of your creator, who we thought was God Yahweh, but here he is saying that you are the child of Lucifer, the devil, and God Satan, as these three people are the same entity. The God that you believe to be good and righteous is evil; and the God that you believe to be evil and destructive, is good: they are apposite = one in the same, and interchangeable. If the almighty God Yahweh created us as the story entails, we are children of God Yahweh, who could very well be the devil but is passing the position on someone else. Do you see the confusion?

In addition, God Satan became in charge of the earth at this point after tempting Adam and Eve, as (KJV)-2 Corinthians 4:4; calls God Satan; "the god of this world". The story goes that God Satan hates us and God Yahweh loves us, but at this point, I cannot tell which is which. Because of Yahweh's selfishness, you go through life the way you do, and he did not stand up for you from the start. That is not love, and the good God Yahweh is not a loving entity. If Adam had eaten from the "tree of life", there would have been;

- peace and tranquility immediately
- direct communication with God Yahweh, (as Adam and Eve had in the Garden before their fall from grace.)
- rest, a body of no diseases, and comfort
- no worries, or misunderstandings, and tension
- no wars and destruction

## **The cycle of 7,000-year plan**

The Gods are big on numbers. You can trace back on everything they do, it is by the numbers. Don't believe me, go research for yourself. Seven is considered to be the perfect number, as there are seven days in a week. Twelve is expressed as being whole or complete; we have 12 months in a year. I can go on and on, you get the idea. Here is something interesting though, the number of man is the number six. For two reasons, it is an imperfect number and the number six in the Bible is directly related to man and his imperfections and shortcomings, again reminding us that we are not perfect. The King James Version, New Living Translation, New American Bible, International Children's Bible, New International Version, etc. etc. etc., all have sixty-six chapters in them. I thought this was a very compelling count as we all have heard of the number 666. Could God Satan be the creator, as it has already named you a child of Satan?

The world was designed for a continuous 7,000-year life cycle. Man was given 6,000-years to rule over himself, and then a 1,000-year reign under Jesus Christ. Why give man 6,000 years to rule over himself; because God Yahweh wanted to show how bad of a job man can do policing himself, therefore needing the direction and guidance of himself. The good God's direction is not so spectacular either, why would you give a murderer a loaded gun, when you already know what he or she will do with it. In this case, our God gave us the loaded gun fully knowing what we would do and how we would act. We are not doing so great, but we will not be doing any better by the hand of God either.

(KJV)-2 Peter 3:8 says; "With the lord, a day is like a thousand years, and a thousand years are like a day." If you believe in the savior named Jesus Christ, he died in the year 3,967, roughly; living only 33 years on the earth. We are roughly in the year 2021 as I write this, but who says this is accurate, as our ancestors did not concern themselves of keeping track of time to the second. It was not that important to them. Anyhow, if this is the case, we are very close to the end of the 6,000-year rule of man. However, hold on, Jesus Christ will have his own reign of terror in the near future. Jesus will reign for 1,000 years after coming back to the earth. All of this just seems like a waste of time and energy, because if you do believe in a one true God; this God has allowed his creation to go through intense amounts of pain and suffering, for his selfishness, just to say that he is the almighty.

In my studies, I observed that these 7,000 years are a repetitive cycle to the Gods; because we have discovered fossils and other items that claim to be millions of years old. (KJV)- Genesis 4:10-14 says; "the lord said, 'what have you done? Listen! Your brother's blood cries out to me from the ground. Now you are under a curse and driven from the ground, which opened its mouth to receive your brother's blood from your hand. When you work the ground, it will no longer yield its crops for you. You will be a restless wanderer on the earth." Cain said to the lord, "My punishment is more than I can bear. Today you are driving me from the land, and I will be hidden from your presence. I will be a restless wanderer on the earth, and whoever finds me will kill me." Whom is Cain talking about in this verse, 'whoever finds me will kill me," after killing his brother Abel? According to scripture, Adam, Eve, Cain, and Abel were the only persons living on the earth as the Gods created them in the Garden of Eden. Is there, was there someone else out there in the world that Cain knew about and was afraid that they would kill him for murdering his brother; could your God have lied to you again?

I believe that when God Yahweh brings heaven to earth and sends everyone else to hell: after Jesus's thousand-year reign, God Yahweh goes back to heaven upstairs and starts the world all over again. Moreover, you have people left over on the earth from the last 7,000-year cycle. It is a cycle that they use, continuously, forever and ever. The Gods keep using the same earth, restoring it, to cycle through and through human beings, the idea being quantity over quality. There could be Nonillions, or Sexdecillion, and even Novemdecillion's of people that lived on this rock that we call home for the moment. God started a new man, named Adam, and put him in a Garden away from the rest, and this man still sinned, therefore, God released him into the wild, with the rest of the world. This is all a game, a game that the Gods plays, trying to find out, who will worship each one unconditionally, with no faults.

| Name of Number | Number of zeros |
|---|---|
| Ten | 1 |
| Hundred | 2 |
| Thousand | 3 |
| Ten thousand | 4 |
| Hundred thousand | 5 |
| Million | 6 |
| Billion | 9 |
| Trillion | 12 |
| Quintillion | 18 |
| Sextillion | 21 |
| Septillion | 24 |
| Octillion | 27 |
| Nonillion | 30 |
| Decillion | 33 |
| Undecillion | 36 |
| Duodecillion | 39 |
| Tredecillion | 42 |
| Quattuordecillion | 45 |

| Quindecillion | 48 |
| Sexdecillion | 51 |
| Septen-decillion | 54 |
| Octodecillion | 57 |
| Novemdecillion | 60 |
| Vigintillion | 63 |
| Centillion | 66 |

## **An epiphany**

I was given visions to see into our physical and invisible "spiritual" world. One of the most aggravating things to me is when the Gods, the creators of the heavens and the earth, pretend to be the good guy, when they are in fact, the bad guys. Who is more to blame for the way the world is, for our human sufferings; humanity or Yahweh or Satan? I blame the Gods for this horrible world we live in, not human beings. Satan will always be who he is, a wretched God, full of hate and envy towards anyone and everything in the world, according to scripture. However, consider for a moment, who God

The tree of Life and the tree of Death.

Yahweh is. God Yahweh claims to be the 'alpha and the omega, the first and the last, the beginning and the end' according to (KJV)-Revelation 22:13. If this is true, then every feeling, emotion, concept, and thought, (good or bad), came from God Yahweh's being. The Gods can blame us for being evil, but <u>in reality</u>, it came from them.

Would we all agree that everyone has their own individual and personal characteristics in this world, and no one was designed the same. That is easy, right. The obvious is repeated because I am by no means trying to convince whoever is reading this to believe in something, I am simply explaining and putting the information out there to be accessible for you. If you are a believer in one God, great, more power to you, but am sorry to say to you, that a lot of information was lied about, and kept from us, and unless you know how to decode the bible, you are missing a mass amount of important messages. Deep down, he hates you, and does not care where you end up.

> Feelings = Mind
> Emotions = Body
> Thoughts = Brain
> Prerogatives = Functioning

Not every person is willing to stand up for what is right, some would prefer to keep quiet and keep their thoughts and beliefs to themselves and go about their business and not stir up any trouble; a slave. This was more common in earlier times, as now the new age movement has taken its place in our society, and more and more protests take place in our culture than ever before. But just because you protest something doesn't mean you know what you are talking about, to protest and argue an argument, you must know the issue from point A to point Z, and not overlook what was covered in point M. (QUR)-Man 76:1-4; "Has there come upon man a period of time when he was nothing to be mentioned? We created man from a liquid mixture, to test him, and we made him hearing and seeing. We guided him on the way, be he appreciative or depreciative. We have prepared for the faithless, chains, yokes, and a searing fire."

Our meaningless lives are just a contest between the two Gods.

# ADDENDUM

## **Example on how to decipher scripture correctly**

This book was written to help you become aware of the truth, what is genuinely out in the world, and to somehow aid you in your journey called life; not going to deep into subjects, but introducing matters that need to be lifted out of the valley. One element that I will leave you with, is how to interpret bible verses. The verse that I chose comes from (KJV)- Psalm 23:4 and is used very often as people see it as a protection device from God Yahweh. It reads as, "Even though I walk through the valley of the shadow of death, I will fear no evil, for you are with me; your rod and your staff, they comfort me." Let me break it down so you can see how to comprehend these verses in the future: first, you are always in the 'valley of the shadow of death', your life can be taken from you in one swift instance (a car wreck, falling, a stray bullet) this is something you can never escape and have no control over; secondly, 'I will fear no evil', your God Yahweh is the definition of true evil, (as the bible tells you he is the one you should fear; as God Satan does not have the authority to send you to hell, take your life or harm you in any manner unless God Yahweh says it is okay. It is God Yahweh and his son Yahshua who hold this jurisdiction over you; third, 'for you are with me', God Yahweh is not with you. (KJV)-Ephesians 1:11 says; "In him we were also chosen, having been predestined according to the plan of him who works out everything in conformity with the purpose of his will." The Gods have a plan for this world, and if you are not a part of it, he is not with you, you are on your own, and all of this has been predestined; a rod and staff is used to steer something straight or back in line, with force, then it says that the rod comforts you. How can you be comforted when you are being beaten? Here, David is saying that he enjoys and is comforted when God Yahweh strikes him, makes him suffer, sends trouble his way, David finds comfort in this. Can anyone else see that all of this is clinically insane. (KJV)-Matthew 5:8 tells us; "Blessed are the pure in heart, for they will see God." For what he really and truly is.

## Four Step Process of Understanding Scripture

1. Word Focus; Focus on what the words really say.
2. Word Relations; How does it relate to you!
3. Context; what are your circumstances in any event or dilemma that can be assessed?
4. Reality; Scripture says one thing, but what does reality tell you.

I firmly believe that if everyone looked the same, had the same things, the world would be a much, much better place. Then no one could ever be jealous, envious, hateful, spiteful and act devious towards another for anything; whether it be for love, jobs, money, or material items. It can be a beautiful thing when someone loves you and you love someone, but how can you absolutely be sure that the person loves you for you and not what you can do and provide for them? Obviously your loving God does not feel the same way.

# DAY 4: STAGE 4

Here are your Gods at their finest.

Heaven equals work; hell equals torment, so what is the difference? You will always be controlled in some fashion or another, whether here on earth, or in heaven or hell; so get used to the idea. All this life is; is just a game (QUR)-The Sovereignty 67:2; He who created life and death, to test you, as to which of you is better in conduct." Who will be a slave and who will not. There are a million and one books out there, telling you about how great God is; you finally have someone that is not afraid of God and that is telling you the truth about his history. As history has always shown, we as human beings, as smart as we think we are; only comprehend a small piece of a subject and not understand the meaning 100 percent. We read and perceive what we want to foresee. We think we know and have the answer to everything, when in fact, you know nothing. Do you actually think that the good God Yahweh is ever going to take your pain and hurt away: that is never going to happen. The Adam and Eve story shows God Yahweh as an immoral bad parent, not as a loving God. The immoral doctrine of original sin, where children are punished for the sins of their parents is hardly the scheme of a moral god. Adam and Eve were punished with casualty, agony, adversity and caused the evil for all of humanity. They themselves 'sinned' before they even knew what the difference between good and evil was. God is immoral: as he punishes you, an innocent person, for sins you did not understand and commit yet. Let me be the first to tell you, heaven will be no different from hell. Hallmark, movies, and poems characterize heaven as little baby angels sitting on clouds all calm, cool and collected. The fact of the matter is; you were never intended to be in heaven with God, if you were, you would be there already. If the life we are living today were never a smooth ride, what would make you think that the next one will? I do not know about you, but I see a person or entity for who and what they are by their actions, not by their words; quoting that old saying 'actions speak louder than words'. You will be doing hard work in heaven, similar to earth; and tormented in hell, pain forever. This life and the afterlife is a no win situation for us human beings.

## **The Truth about Heaven**

Humility, kindness, temperance, chastity, patience, charity, and diligence are the seven holy virtues of heaven, but your God Yahweh does not even practice these details towards you. The loving God and the angels are currently in heaven, while we are here on earth. Make no mistake about it: you will be controlled in heaven. Based on the way he treats his beloved creation, man, with the history of violence and sin, and his condemnation; very few souls will enjoy this place called heaven. (KJV)-Revelation 21:1-8 says; "Then I saw 'a new heaven and a new earth,' for the first heaven and the first earth had passed away, and there was no longer any sea. I saw the Holy City, the new Jerusalem, coming down out of heaven from God, prepared as a bride beautifully dressed for her husband. And I heard a loud voice from the throne saying, "Look! God's dwelling place is now among the people, and he will dwell with them. They will be his people, and God himself will be with them and be their God. "He will wipe every tear from their eyes. There will be no more death' or mourning or crying or pain, for the old order of things has passed away." He who was seated on the throne said, "I am making everything new!" Then he said, "Write this down, for these words are trustworthy and true." He said to me: "It is done. I am the Alpha and the Omega, the beginning and the end. To the thirsty I will give water without cost from the spring of the water of life. Those who are victorious will inherit all this, and I will be their God and they will be my children. But the cowardly, the unbelieving, the vile, the murderers, the sexually immoral, those who practice magic arts, the idolaters and all liars—they will be consigned to the fiery lake of burning sulfur. This is the second death."

The Gods will let mankind destroy itself, as we are already doing: all for a dollar bill. The antichrist will come to the earth first performing miracles as if he was Jesus Christ. You think that your life is terrible now, the seven years before Jesus's second coming will be like nothing you have ever seen before, apocalypse movies from Hollywood will seem like a walk in the park. Remember, the Gods proceed in numbers. Jesus will come for the second time, to clean the mess up, and what will truthfully happen is, God Yahweh will bring heaven down to earth, and remake this world, supposedly restoring all that man has destroyed and making Jerusalem, his capital city, as Israel is his already chosen nation from the inauguration. Trust me, when I honestly say to you, that God Yahweh never wanted you; never cared for you, never showed concern for you, never wanted you to succeed, and never showed any interest for your wants and needs. Heaven will be imported down to our lowly presence, where he will dwell with you, never has the plan been for you to go there, as you were led to believe and trust, it is only offered. Your destiny has always been to live and stay on this planet.

Then a thousand-year reign of Jesus Christ will take place on earth with God Yahweh in the tabernacle in Jerusalem, with God Satan locked in hell for this period of time. After this duration is over, God Yahweh will go back to heaven and bring the few souls that he wants with him in heaven that have done good deeds: the ones that are deemed worthy enough to be in heaven. The rest of humanity will remain on earth until death, or go to hell and you will not exist any longer. Remember, I said that this is a system to them, after the

You are not special: Heaven will be no different than earth.

7,000-year period is over; it starts all over again, letting Satan out and allowing

the world to progress again. 6,000 years of man ruling himself, then 1,000 years of Jesus Christ's reign. Do you remember Cain telling God Yahweh that he was scared to be forced out of the Garden of Eden because there were already people out there that he was afraid of: the remaining people from this process are the ones already present that he mentioned.

If you are expecting to sit back, calm and relaxed for all of eternity in heaven; that is not the case my friends, he will be putting you to work, and his claim is that you will never grow weary or tired, like you do here. I ask because it says the <u>work</u> will be joyful and not burdensome in heaven, but again, can you really believe what he says after lying to you for so long. We are his slaves, always have been, and that is what you will be in heaven, humans were always lied to about their purpose. (QUR)-The Heifer 2:29 says; "It is He who created for you everything on earth, then turned to the heaven, and made them seven heavens. And He is aware of all things." There are seven levels in heaven, but scripture is contradictory, as it says that works do not save you, you are saved by faith; but why does God Yahweh uses your works on earth to incorporate your place, promotion, and status in heaven by levels of authority and positions. Essentially, if you make it to heaven, people who have been more courteous, kinder, considerate, and exceptional than you on earth, will rule over you, and watch over you to make sure you are doing what you are supposed to be doing. My friends, this is just another example of enslavement. You cannot win. In heaven, you can be cast down to hell, just as the angels were; with one slip up of the tongue, or disobedience towards God Yahweh.

Everyone will be wearing crowns in heaven, but the superior ones will have more jewelry and rubies on their crown to point out greater works performed on earth. The 24 elders will be over everyone and down goes the chain of command from here; similar to the pyramid scheme we have working out in earth's businesses. Here is the sad part, you will still be doing work in heaven but; it will supposedly be joyful, since you are in the presence of God. (KJV)-Revelation 22:3 says; "No longer will there be any curse. The throne of God and of the Lamb will be in the city, and his servants will serve him." You will still have to grow food, and drink water, and everything that you are doing today; you just will never grow weary or tired like we do here. So I say, what is the enjoyment of heaven if we will be doing the exact same things that we are now? Working, never relaxed, and always on the move, this is the type of actions we carry out on earth.

Jesus Christ is currently sitting at the right had of Yahweh, waiting to devour you like a lion and send you to hell for those who did not believe, have faith, and did not show trust in him during his second coming to earth. How can you trust an entity like this? This clearly shows three domineering, controlling, autocrats. This is not love. Love is showing forgiveness no matter what someone does. These entities do not present love; they present a give and take scenario, you believe in me and ask for forgiveness, then I will forgive you. Nobody told you how life was going to be this way, but I am telling you.

## The Truth about Hell

Some people say it is a folklore tale for the damned. I am here to tell you, it is not a tale; it is real, and it is awful and dreadful. It is managed by the evil God; Satan. Hell has nothing to do with being hot, sweaty, or with flames. It is more of an emotional dilemma. You already know what it is like to be sad, lonely, deprived, depressed, full of lust, hate and envy: this is how it will be, forever. Here is the truth, you are in hell right now. There is no place underneath the earth or imaginary spot. This is hell. People love their sins and the world so much, that they will never relinquish it. The congregation of souls in hell will forever look up and see what they have always longed for, aspired for, but cannot obtain from the ones who do make it to heaven above..

(QUR)-The Constellations 85:10; "Those who tempt the believers, men and women, then do not repent, for them is the punishment of hell; for them is the punishment of burning." But who is the true tempter? It is not God Satan; it is God Yahweh. I am not tempting you, I am simply laying out the facts for you. Now please take in mind, that the purpose of hell was a place specifically designed for demons. Yes, there are angels and demons walking around the existing earth in the spiritual world that you cannot see. But God Yahweh is happy, content, and pleased to place you there for not being able to follow his commandments. (KJV)-2 Peter 2:4 says; "For if God spared not the angels that sinned, but cast them down to hell, and delivered them into chains of darkness, to be reserved unto judgment", and he will do the same to you. It is impossible for human beings not to sin, your God Yahweh knows this; but says in (KJV)-Romans 6:23; "for the wages of sin is death." Yahweh still condemns you and the punishment for sin is death. Eternal life is a gift, which we do not have unless God gives it to us. You can be the best person in the world, and God Yahweh will still not let you into the gates of heaven. So, why would he send you to a place designed for more torture and suffering than the one you previously had, all for the faith in a person named Jesus Christ? The conviction is that, no matter how much evil you have done in your life, you can be pardoned and go to heaven with asking Jesus Christ for forgiveness and believing that he died on the cross for your sins. Here we go with the control issue again. Why is there only one option? A person can spend their whole life being a good person, helping others, then have one accident, die before asking for forgiveness, and he or she is in hell. If you stick to what the truth says, and what you feel in your heart, you will find everything you need to know. Common sense goes a long way.

There are seven deadly sins in the world; 1-pride, (being the most severe), envy, gluttony, lust, wrath, greed, and 7-sloth, (the least severe), in this order. In addition, every sin committed can be placed into one of these seven categories. I have never been to hell, but assuming the importance of these sins, it is easy to conclude that there are nine levels of hell and punishment is handed down according to severity. I assume the number nine, to mock Jesus' spirits of the heart which are = love, joy, peace, patience, kindness, goodness, faithfulness, gentleness, and self-control. The evil characteristics opposite of the nine fruits of the spirit are; enmity, sorrow, anxiety/worry, Impatience/vengeance, harshness, immorality, distrust, self-ego, incontinence.

9 levels of hell's sufferings
First level – limbo – least suffering in hell's regards
Second level – lust
Third level – gluttony
Fourth level - greed
Fifth level – anger/wrath
Sixth level – Heresy
Seventh level – Violence
Eighth level – Fraud
Ninth level – Treachery – most suffering in hell's regards

(KJV)-Luke 12:47-48 says; "The servant who knows the master's will and does not get ready or does not do what the master wants will be beaten with many blows. However, the one who does not know and does things deserving punishment will be beaten with few blows. From everyone who has been given much, much will be demanded; and from the one who has been entrusted with much, much more will be asked". Here is a loving

God who is actually okay with beating you, where Satan will torment and antagonize you to no avail. (KJV)-Matthew 7:13-14 says; "Wide is the gate and broad is the road that leads to destruction, and many enter through it. But small is the gate and narrow the road that leads to life and only a few find it". God Yahweh is okay with 75 percent of the world going in hell, and he living in a place called heaven without them. Is this love? Could he have done more to show that he cares about you? Once again, you be the judge about the entity that created you.

Friends, I am 41 years old as I write this in 2021; and I do not have the strength or energy to worry about this anymore. This life just beats you, chews you up, spits you out, and I am tired of it, tired of God Yahweh and God Satan's games. Why should you stick up for a God that never stood up for you? God Yahweh expects you to protect his name, all the while, 'smearing yours'. Remember, he has the nerve to say that life is not fair. The good God Yahweh wants you to take headaches, punishment, grief, and agony; and still keep your head held high. Scripture says that believing in Jesus Christ is all you have to do, but God Yahweh always has tricks up his sleeve to keep you out of heaven. He will look at what you have done upon the earth, and some sins are unforgivable, so yes, you can believe in Christ, and still not get into the gates.

The word 'hell' is never mentioned in the bible. Instead the word 'hades' is used. Same thing, but just showing the difference in words and pronunciation. When hell shows up in some English bibles, it is translating the word gehenna, the name of a valley outside the walls of the city Jerusalem. People used to sacrifice idols there. God Yahweh will keep sinners alive forever in Hades; not to punish, but to allow you to reconcile to him. Wow, what an evil God. He will keep you in hell until you say 'I have had enough God, please take me out, I will obey!' God is a control freak, and since he cannot control your every action, your destiny is Hades. But you will not suffer forever. You will be destroyed. It is the destruction, not the suffering, that lasts forever.

# DAY 5: STAGE 5

How do you get to know these entities with minimal supervision?

I was chosen to write this to you: I do not know how you feel, but I am exhausted behind this world, these gods, and humanity. A god that answers to no one is untrustworthy: it is dangerous, unstable, uncertain and vulnerable of itself. It does not care about itself, why would it care about you: you should never have to beg, but you do. Life is not exciting, it never was; it was always designed to be hard and stressful, you should stop looking for the next best thing (because it is not coming) and just accept what is in front and back of you. Scripture tells us that we were made and created to know who God is; and my friends, deep down in your heart and soul, you already know who he is, and you do not need to read the scriptures. But as (QUR)-The Family of Imran 3:17 says to you; "He specifies His mercy for whomever he wills." If he does not like you or you are not part of his will, God Yahweh can care less about who you are and your circumstances. The good God Yahweh says that his works are all around us; "you see me in the world". Yes, I see the stars, clouds and the sky, rain, snow, the ground, trees, the sun and the moon; but I also see hunger, poverty, people addicted to dependents, brokenness, loneliness, fighting, killing, stealing, lying, corruption, kids disrespecting parents and vice versa. The latter is the good God Yahweh I see and know; a God with all the power in the universe yet allows us to live in this manner and does nothing for us. He just loves to sit on his throne in heaven, and watch us suffer, day in and day out, with no conviction in his heart. It is the good God Yahweh who makes you cry, get into trouble, and make mistakes, all the while; blaming the evil God Satan for the mess that is our world. Satan cannot harm or kill anyone without God's permission. If Satan wants to kill you, all he has to do is ask God Yahweh, and, there you have it, you either stay alive or are dead. I discuss the more indebt story of Job in chapter twenty-three regarding this subject.

People of ancient times and modern day were no fools. Human beings have always worshiped other idols because they realized that they could not depend on the living Gods to provide for their needs. Therefore, they looked elsewhere. The good God Yahweh and evil God Satan have no one to blame but themselves for humanity turning their backs on them. This is the fault of the Gods creating something that can think and act for itself; free will, according to God, and something that they could not control. I am by no means a fan of the evil God Satan; but it irks me when I hear someone say 'be good or the devil is going to get you', my friends, it is not him who you have to fear, it is your loving good God Yahweh-father of Jesus Christ who you should fear. The good God Yahweh is the one who lies, is demanding, possesses the 'it's my way or the highway' attitude, and will let Satan have you for misbehaving.

In your eyes, sin is pleasant and good; it is fun and makes you feel satisfied. The good God Yahweh does not want you to sin. "What is good for you, he considers bad; and what is bad, he considers good". A bit of a tongue twister, but read it again, and it will make perfect sense to you. The Wachowski brothers, now transgender women, who wrote and produced the movie 'The Matrix', got it right. I discuss the matrix in stage twenty-nine. We are living in a fantasy world called the matrix where you can make things, see and interact with objects, all the while two Gods who do not give a damn about you or your family are watching behind the scenes, and despise you and really want to harm you. One mistake lies in trying to learn whom the God's are from theology, priests, pastors and other people. How is someone else going to teach you who God is when he or she does not know exactly who they are? Only you know who your God is, or Gods are. People who claim to know God say things such as,

1. *Those who know God have great energy for God*.

The fire always burns out, just as the sun will. Take yourself for example; the second you were born is the second your body started to die, deteriorating, and death is coming for you and you can do nothing to stop it. I know it is hard for you to except the things I am telling you, but the sooner you realize that this life is a waste, the better off you will be. You may see a newborn baby as life, fresh, and the latest; but in God's eye, he or she is already on the hit list. I have met countless people who were into the loving God Yahweh, and then a few years later, they have moved on from that passion and dedication; on to something else. Why is this? Because your creator God does not deliver: you are presenting emotions and warmth towards him, but you are not receiving the same in return. We wait and wait to hear and feel something to happen from him, and it never does. I personally feel that the prophets who helped write the bible did so out of fear, not love; enslavement. If you are a born again person; the struggles become even greater. When you give your life to God Yahweh, it does not get easier; the struggle becomes even greater and more difficult: as you feel more alone than ever before, where is the common sense in this behavior, teaching, and leadership?

2. *Those who know God have great thoughts of God.*

I disagree, and you do as well. Most of your thoughts are not about God, they are about getting the light bill paid, food and clothing taken care of, and why did he allow this to happen to me. You spend more time worrying about why this or that happened in your life instead of waiting on a blessing. It is because deep down, you realize and know that the blessing will never come through. Why do you keep trusting in a God that brings broken promises? How can you have loving thoughts about an entity that puts you through the drama of daily life, and even years? The Gods say that we are their greatest achievement; can you tell?

3.  *Those who know God show great boldness for God.*

The opposite is true. People do not fight for God Yahweh because they know that this God never fought for them. No one has the time or energy to worship, please, give thanks to a God as their lives are too busy and unfulfilled. People speak boldly of him when times are good, but when times get bad; those same persons for God have shut mouths and kick him to the curb. People of the clergy are supposed to be the ones that know God the best; but look at how they fill about their own selfish desires and motives. Story after story of these clergymen doing horrible and filthy things to people that show trust and faith in them. I am talking about men and women of all religions and cults. When will it end?

4.  *Those who know God have great contentment for God.*

If you claim to have great contentment in God, why are you living in a faith filled with worry, doubt, and frustration? Christians, catholics, baptists, and congregations of all other religions who have lived good lives; are afraid that they will not make it into the gates of heaven. This is the God you serve; a God that you can never satisfy with your faith, works, and prayers. He always finds something to chastise you for. Your position in him should be built on stout bricks and stones. However, at the same time, this God Yahweh gives you the feeling of 'nothing is ever good enough'. Someone born into poverty or financial hardship does not see this God Yahweh in the same light as someone who is in a better monetary state. Your position in life dictates your love towards him. When he does good things for you, you love him: when he does bad things to you, you hate him.

Knowing God is the worst thing that you can try to do in your life. You do not want to really know what this entity is really like, and he does not want the truth to be unveiled. Lucky for you, that meaningful task fell on my hands, and you can find out all you need to know right here. The loving God has put the information out there in things such as the bible, and other lost writings, but no one has an interest to read them anymore. I say agian, but even back when before Jesus was born, citizens of the world never cared about God Yahweh or cared to learn more. I believe this is because God Yahweh and God Satan takes humanity for a bunch of fools. In his mind, he expects worship and praise for giving us this world. In our mind, we say, worship and praise you for what: a world filled with hardships, cruelty, loneliness, strife, hunger, sadness, abandonment, strain, and corruption with no sign of relief and comfort. We are and have been on separate pages from the beginning, so how can we ever get it right?

From the (QUR)-The Table 5:27-31, the story of Cain and Abel says; "And relate to them the true story of Adam's two sons, (Cain and Abel) when they offered an offering to God Yahweh, and it was accepted from one of them, but it was not accepted from the other. Cain said, "I will kill you." Abel said, "God accepts only from the righteous. If you extend your hand to kill me, I will not extend my hand to kill you; for I fear God, Lord of the Worlds. I would rather you bear my sin and your sin, and you become among the inmates of the Fire. Such is the reward for the evildoers." Then Cain's soul prompted him to kill his brother, so he killed him, and became one of the losers. Then God Yahweh sent a raven digging the ground, to show him how to cover his brother's corpse. Cain said, "Woe to me, I am unable to be like this raven, and bury my brother's corpse." So he became full of regrets."

The Gods and you have two different sets of ideas on what this world is and should be.

# DAY 6: STAGE 6

Why does the good God make you cry, when he claims to love you?

Every person, at one point in his or her life, has sat down somewhere or another and asked himself or herself the question, "There has to be more to this life than this." I hate to be the bearer of bad news; but no, there is not more to this world than what it is. I have even asked myself this same question many times over, and have come up with the same answer repeatedly. I came up with the phrase, "We are born, live an odious existence, and then die!" From my experience, and yours as well, the little joy and happiness that we are exposed to is nothing in comparison to the affliction and bruised spirits that we end up with. Some lives are too far gone to ever come back to God Yahweh or Jesus Christ because of this. The truth is that your life on this earth is the trial period for a place that you will spend eternity in. Your life was decided for you ahead of time and over something, you had no control over. This is your punishment for Adam and Eve making the wrong decision on which tree to eat from. In addition, as I said earlier, the good God did no justice in informing them what life could have been like by eating from the correct tree. Let me point out a few realities:

1. God never needed you
2. God lied about your existence
3. God did not create you because he was lonely
4. You were made for God's pleasure, not yours
5. God does not need the earth
6. God does not need your worship and praise
7. God does not need your money.

Do you really think that these supreme beings needed something as simple as you? We humans, made of flesh and bone, with simplistic thoughts and ideas, the barbaric way of discarding waste, and the vile process of participating in sexual motives. No they did not, they never needed us. Humans naturally want to hold themselves to intelligent, complex standards; but this is highly incorrect. Simplicity works because humans are simple creatures that desire simple purposes. It is not that hard to study human nature and see that all comes down to a very primitive and simple desire of trying to understand a complex universe that their tiny minds can never grasp. Simplicity itself is tracked down to primitive warfare used by cavemen so they can gain a competitive edge over another caveman for survival. That is exactly what we are still doing currently in our modern age, in the form of the same word: war!

I know people love to be prideful and say that 'I am control of my life'. No, you are not, if the Gods took the breath and air out of your lungs, you would cease to exist. (KJV)-Isaiah 41:10 says; "So do not fear, for I am with you; do not be dismayed, for I am your God. I will strengthen you and help you; I will uphold you with my righteous right hand." Moreover, many things are out of control in your life, but you are too audacious to admit it. What we are dealing with down here is two players controlling the joystick on a PlayStation 4, and we are the game.

*Monotheism:* the doctrine or belief that there is only one God.

*Atheist:* a person who disbelieves or lacks belief in the existence of God or Gods.

*Agnostic:* a person who believes that nothing is known or can be known of the existence or nature of God or of anything beyond material phenomena; a person who claims neither faith nor disbelief in God.

*Polytheism:* is the worship or belief in multiple deities, which are assembled into a pantheon of Gods and goddesses, along with their own religions and rituals.

## First Book of Adam and Eve

Adam and Eve were supposedly living in a glorious place in the beginning called the "Garden of Eden": but according to whom? However, the good God Yahweh blamed them so much for choosing the way of the evil God, supposedly, the way of sin; that instead of forgiving them, the good God Yahweh kicked them out of the garden. In this particular book, it tells the life of Adam and Eve's experiences after they were thrown out of the Garden of Eden, the world we know today. They went from being in the presence of God and lying around all day; to having to toil and slave for their food and clothing. Even they came to hate this world so immensely, in a short period of time; that they tried to committed suicide.

In Pseudepiprapha, book of Adam and Eve, 21:1-9 tells; "Then Adam and Eve went in search of the garden. And the heat beat like a flame on their faces; and they sweated from the heat, and cried before the Lord God. But the place where they cried was close to a high mountain, facing the western gate of the garden. Then Adam threw himself down from the top of that mountain; his face was torn and his flesh was ripped; he lost a lot of blood and was close to death. Meanwhile Eve remained standing on the mountain crying over him, thus lying. In addition, she said, "I don't wish to live after him; for all that he did to himself was through me. Then she threw herself after him; and was torn and ripped by stones; and remained lying as dead. But the merciful God, who looks over His creatures, looked at Adam and Eve as they lay dead, and he sent his word to them, and raised them. In addition, said to Adam, "O Adam, all this misery which you have brought on yourself, will have no affect against my rule, neither will it alter the covenant of the 500 years." Adam died from this event, but God sent an angel to revive him. Telling him that his time was not done yet, and so he and Eve, continued on with their lives, in agony and discomfort.

Here are five basic truths, five foundation principles of the knowledge about God which Christians have, and has determined our course of history, throughout. They are as follows:

1. **God has spoken to man, and the Bible is his Word, given to us to make us wise unto salvation.**

    Yes, the bible is God's word, which makes it all the scarier. Those actions are definitely speaking loud and clear as the wicked prospers; and the righteous suffers. You would think that if you were a child of Yahweh God that you would have the best advantages; but the opposite is true. When you are a person trying to leave your old ways behind, and do things the good God's way; more trials and tribulations become your way of survival. People make promises and say things that they have no intention of keeping on a daily basis. Words are cheap, anyone can tell another that they love them, but they will never feel the immensity of affection and care until it is acted upon in the proper manner. We are here fighting and scratching for survival on the planet, and where are your Gods? You can tell someone you love him or her as many times as you want, but until your behavior coincides with it, the other person will probably never believe you. I feel that the Gods hate you and I; and I wrote this knowing I am not the only one feeling this way. I have been yearning to see love shown to me from the good God Yahweh: and am still waiting!

2. **God is Lord and King over his world; he rules all things for his own glory, displaying his perfections in all that he does, in order that men and angels may worship and adore him.**

    First, which God are we talking about? Mentioned earlier in stage three, God Satan is in charge of this world that you live in now, runs everything in it: the systems of government, hollywood, business, and sports, etc. This shows how much your loving good God Yahweh loves you, by giving total control and authority to God Satan instead of Jesus Christ. God Yahweh gave up on you a long, long time ago and wanted no part of this any longer. Why should you love him? If anyone is showing interest, it is God Satan. (KJV)-Daniel 4:35 says to us; "All the inhabitants of the earth are accounted as nothing. He does according to his will in the host of heaven and among the inhabitants of earth; and no one can ward off his hand or say to him, "What have you done?" The people that believe in going to heaven really do not love God Yahweh; they do so out of fear.

3. **God is Savior, active in sovereign love through the Lord Jesus Christ to rescue believers from the guilt and power of sin, to adopt them as his children and to bless them accordingly.**

If there were one almighty God, he would have never allowed sin to enter the world, keeping it away, because he is all powerful and loves you; thus, keeping peace on earth for all of eternity, if he was good. The obvious fact that you experience pain, unhappiness and suffering proves three things.

1- God allowed sin to enter the world on purpose; it was not by accident.
2- That one God does not control everything.
3- That God loves to see you go through what you go through.

The gods where bored, so they created us to have something to do and keep themselves occupied. The Gods did not create you out of love, as is their claim. You must love yourself, as no one else will.

4. **God is triune; there are within the Godhead three persons, the Father, the Son and the Holy Spirit and the work of salvation is one in which all three act together, the Father purposing redemption, the Son securing it and the Spirit applying it.**

If this was a special event, why does God Yahweh and God Satan each have Godheads of their own? Each has a plan for this world, but God Yahweh has given up the fight where God Satan has not. The story tells that Yahweh will win the battle at Armageddon, but is he really winning? When 3/4 of the world is going to hell, and only 1/4 is going to heaven, I see this as a win for Satan. He has definitely won the popularity and number of soul's contest. More importantly, the whole point of this experiment was to obtain as many souls as possible in their individual place of eternity. Remember, it is a contest between the two, at your dispense. No one wants to be used, but it is your life. They use you for their benefit and do not care how it gets done.

5. **Godliness means responding to God's revelation in obedience and trust, worship and faith, prayer and praise, service and submission. Life must be seen and lived in the light of God's Word.**

Man and woman have never seen the world in the same eyes as the Gods has; this is because we are not the same kind of creature. How can you expect to get along with someone when we are not made up of the same ideas, material, wants, and needs? He looks at this world as beautiful; but it is not. And again, he wants you to submit to his will, not yours. Doesn't this make you angry? He expects you to live for him and not for yourself: and he calls us selfish. We are not here to live for God; we are here to live for ourselves, because if we do not take care of ourselves, who else will? He claims that you have free will; yet is adamant in controlling you. I hope that I can help you learn how to read the bible better and learn the meaning of these all so important messages. This is a God who created you, but yet does not want you to enjoy yourself and be happy and does not give you the tools to make your happiness a reality.

## Secret Meetings

I have a correction for you: it is not the early bird who gets the worm; it is the bird that steals the worm from another and gets away with it. Everything in this world is backwards, couldn't you tell by now? The God that you recognize as love is evil; and the God that you recognize as evil is love. The supposedly good one is trying to show you how evil the other one is: and the supposedly evil one is trying to show you what a liar, a fraud, and not of love, the other one is.

These two Gods have many, many, many private conversations and debates concerning your life amongst themselves. They decide whether to kill you or let you live; send a blessing or curse your way; hurt you physically or let you be healthy; make you depressed or happy; make your marriage last or file for divorce, you believe that you are in control of your own destiny: but that is foolish thinking. Someone, somewhere (human beings) in our world is and has been in communication with these Gods, directing and manipulating where the next steps are in our growth, technology, and progressions have gone. The Gods are the controllers and you are the game. Yes, you can decide what you want to do; but it is they who are guiding you along a certain route; and as I have said before, let the chips fall where they may. I really think it is time that we stop worrying about the small things in life; and start asking the bigger questions. It is time to stop being satisfied with just living. Aren't you tired of just waking up to the same bullshit every day?

When I first apprehended this, yes, it made me upset, but you know what it also did for me; it set me free, freer than I have ever been in my life. Once I realized that I could control no one but myself; I released the worry and thought behind trying to please two Gods that can never be pleased or made happy. I stopped caring about the simple-minded activities that man does, and the pathetic motives behind power and money. I realized that I would make the most of the moments that I am here and not worry about the future; because tomorrow is never promised. It is scary, frightening to know that your life is being controlled by another entity. I am telling you this because there is nothing we can do about it; it was the cards we were dealt. There is no winning outcome for humanity. In Pseudepiprapha, book of Adam and Eve, The first sunrise 16:1-13 tells; After this, Adam and Eve continued to stand in the cave, praying and crying, until the morning dawned on them. And when they saw the light returned to them, they retrained from fear, and strengthened their hearts. Then Adam began to come out of the cave. And when he came to the mouth of it, and stood and turned his face towards the east, and saw the sunrise in glowing rays, and felt the heat thereof on his body, he was afraid of it, and thought in his heart that this flame came forth to plague him. He then cried and beat his chest, then he fell on the ground on his face and made his request, saying: "O Lord, plague me not, neither consume me, nor yet take away my life from the earth." For he thought the sun was God. Because while he was in the garden and heard the voice of God and the sound He made in the garden, and feared Him, Adam never saw the brilliant light of the sun, neither did its flaming heat touch his body. Therefore, he was afraid of the sun when flaming rays of it reached him. He thought God meant to plague him there with all the days He had decreed for him. For Adam also said in his thoughts, as God did not plague us with darkness, behold, He has caused this sun to rise and to plague us with burning heat. But while he was thinking like this in his heart, the Word of God came to him and said: "O Adam, get up on your feet. This sun is not God; but it has been created to give light by day, of which I spoke to you in the cave saying, 'that the dawn would come, and there would be light by day.' But I am God who comforted you in the night." And God ceased to commune with Adam.

Humanity is going nowhere fast.

# DAY 7: STAGE 7
## CURSES

The topic of curses is so grand that I had to put a chapter in this book and another chapter in the second book.

Even Jesus Christ is cursed. He is cursed because he is destined to do what he has already accomplished and what he is still to finish. He did not ask for this. He died on a cross for people who do not give a damn and his next item to finish is sending those of you who do not believe and those who do believe to hell/hades. He was forced to die on the cross by God Yahweh, you think he really wanted to do this? No, he did not. He even asked Yahweh in two separate times why god forsaked him. in (KJV)-Matthew 27:46 and Mark 15:34: "My God, My God, why have you forsaken me?". The first time was when he was first nailed to the cross and the second was when he was about to die and his blood was almost bled out of his body.

Sometimes you wonder how people can be sick and mentally disturbed, but it is easy for me to see: this is the same God that had humanity multiply itself by brothers and sisters, fathers and daughters, mothers and sons having sex in the beginning to get you to where you are now. This creator god Yahweh is a hideous, cruel, obscene, atrocious entity pretending to be of love and compassion. This is the same God that had sex with Mary to conceive Jesus Christ through the spirit. He cannot follow his own rules, so how are you expected to? I am a human being speaking to you, a human being out of love and respect, this god does not do this; he bosses around orders and ultimatums. If this good almighty God Yahweh loved you so much, why does he curse you? You do not make your own destiny, he does it for you! The answer to this question is he curses you so that you can see your mistake and come back to him. How does this make any sense at all?

There are way more than just these ten but I present ten curses you do not know or you do know you are doing. God Yahweh's purpose is not giving you peace of mind but giving you stress and agony.

1.  *Power of the tongue;*

(KJV)-Proverbs 18:21 tells you that; "Death and life are in the power of the tongue and those who love it will eat its fruit." I once heard someone say that it is not gossiping if it is fact: lol, it is considered gossiping regardless if it is fact of fiction. It is people like this that have helped me right these books. The words you speak have power over your blessings or curses and is done according to your faith. Repeated, many of you miss the meaning of scripture even though you read it. This verse is saying that you curse yourself from achieving opportunities of love, financial blessings, healthy children, jobs, inheritances, mental blessings; but do not be deceived, God is waiting for you to mess up because he doesn't want to give these to you to start with.

2.  *The curse of Unforgiveness;*

Someone disrespects you in the slighted instance and you raise hell. You have to remember that moments do not last and five years down the road, you will not even remember what it was about. I have had issues with forgiveness, but I got over it by not caring anymore and just minding my own business; sometimes it is hard but I try my best. Do not go to your grave holding a grudge against someone; it is not worth it, regardless of where you end up.

3.  *Withcraft;*

Believe it or not and you should; sports teams, models, movies, music, commercials, etc. are all forms of witchcraft. Explain to me how you are sitting on the couch lounging and then a burger king or KFC, whatever, they are all the same, commercial comes on and then soon after you are hungry for a super-sized combo or man, I have to get that suv. Times have changed. It is not the old look of boiling pots, flying brooms and crosses; it is modern technology. The Kardashian family is a prime example of modern day witches. Anytime you want to watch something that is full of stupidity and foolishness-(which they are)-you are in a trance state. I am protected because I believe in the real God even though he does not love me. It is something that you just have to except.

4. *Harming the Innocent;*

Innocent people are considered the hidden face of God. According to the loving God, no one is innocent because no one is perfect, so how can you harm the innocent? The innocent would be considered children and mentally retarded who have no idea what the real world consists of. However, this is the same loving god who does not protect them. He puts them in broken families, fake religions, foster homes, single-family homes where they can be sexually, emotionally, and physically molested and abused. Yes, this god is all about love!

5. *Curse over Money;*

Is this a blessing or a curse? You hold onto your money like it is your lifeboat; all the while, God will take it from you in an instance. Once you break a hundred dollar bill, even to buy something that is twenty dollars; that remaining eighty is already spent. The more tightly you hold on to it is the faster it is spent. Most people measure their self-worth by their bank account. The bigger it is, the better they feel about themselves. Because we put so much energy into earning money, it represents the very energy of life as we see it. Some people feel that they and they alone are responsible for their success, that their intelligence and abilities made it so. This is the serious challenge of wealth: to not be deceived by your own ego but to remember that it is G-d who gives you the mind to think and the body to participate in activities. On its own, money can be a curse. Money can cause endless anxiety, for no matter how much you have, you can never be sure that you will not somehow lose it all.

6. *The cost of Anger;*

Holding on to anger can bring on other issues such as sickness, disease and worry. We usually focus on the victims of anger; but what about the ones that are causing it, they are in dire need of help as well. They would not be causing you anger if they were not experiencing it. The whole world is broken and have a god that says he is there to heal and comfort; but where is he? What is your situation?

7. *Curse of Racism;*

This will never go away, even in the year 2500; you are so ignorant. God does not care what skin color you are. Everyone has a color to them, everyone, remember that. The fact that Martin Luther King Jr and others had to go through what they went through is insane. The world has always been divided on Sundays. You are busy worrying about who is wearing what and who is with who, you should be focused on getting your life together. God does not care if you are black, yellow, white, or brown; but you do.

8. *Legalism versus Law;*

Legalism is the dependence on moral law-(yourself)-rather than on religious faith and The law is the ten commandments-(better obey it or else). Just because you believe something is right does not make it right. Legalism is you believing that you will go to heaven because you gave twenty dollars to the man begging on the street corner. The law says you will not get into heaven because you cheated on your wife. No, it is not fair, but who said life was fair? No one did, no one ever said life was fair: and certainly not God Yahweh! The bible/quran never says to confess your sins to a priest or pastor. What it does say is this (KJV)-James 5:16; "Confess your trespasses to one another, and pray for one another; that you may be healed." Confess to the one that you have wronged and forgive one another and Yahweh will forgive you.

9. *Poverty;*

(KJV)-Proverbs 13:22 says; "A good man leaves an inheritance to his children's children, but the wealth of the sinner is stored up for the righteous." In the first part of that verse, how are you supposed to store up wealth for your grandchildren when you are living check to check? In addition, in the second part, when you try to store up on your wealth on earth, it will be given to someone else when you die. The bible reminds you that the only thing that can destroy the promises of God Yahweh is the lack of knowledge or understanding-(KJV)-Hosea 4:6. Poverty is a curse put on you by god Yahweh. Everyone is poor by the simple fact that he owns it all anyway. (KJV)-Psalm 24:1; "The earth is the lord's, and all it contents, the world, and those who dwell in it."

10. *Obeying your father and mother;*

They know more about you than you do. We have all heard of the phrase 'He's a chip off the old block', this is nothing new or 'Like father, like son'. Family history and dna is passed on from one to another; even if you don't want it. Not even Jesus Christ is good, the proof is right here in (KJV)-Matthew 19:16 a rich young ruler asked; "What good thing shall I do that I may have eternal life." (KJV)-Matthew 19:17-18 Jesus replied; "So he said to him, Why do you call me good? No one is good but one, that is God Yahweh. But if you want to enter life, keep the commandments."

A curse (also called a jinx, hex or execration) is any expressed wish that some form of adversity or misfortune will befall or attach to some other entity—one or more persons, a place, or an object. In particular, "curse" may refer to a wish that harm or hurt will be inflicted by any supernatural powers, such as a spell, a prayer, an imprecation, an execration, magic, witchcraft, God, a natural force, or a spirit. In many belief systems, the curse itself (or accompanying ritual) is considered to have some causative force in the result. They are alive and well in this modern day age as they were in the old days. You make me laugh because you do wrong, go to church, and ask or do not ask god to forgive you and expect everything to be fine.

You know, fashion designers, cable news networks, sportscasters, manufacturing products, etc. etc. etc. all try to tell you how to dress, what to believe, and who is important: none of them are important, their lives are even more jacked up than yours. Who the fuck are you anyway? Keep partying, drinking, doing drugs, lying, cheating while your life passes you by.

Look in the mirror and find out who you really are.

# DAY 8: STAGE 8

The loving God Yahweh knew that you could never obey these commandments.

The truth is, he always knew that you would never obey these laws, and that you would always sin; then why would he give them to you in the first place? To start, there were hundreds, even thousands of orders; but you could not even obey ten, so they were minimized. The reason is because God Yahweh wants to prove to you that you are nothing, mean nothing, and that you need him. He wants you to ask him for help and guidance. God wants you to fall, pick yourself up, and ask for direction; what a selfish and narcissistic entity. This is why he puts you through so many predicaments on this planet. And the sad part is; even when some persons humble themselves and actually pray to him for help, he is nowhere to be found, ignoring your partitions, while situations get worse, relationships get out of control, financial obligations get harder, and bitterness runs rampant.

Hunting is the practice of pursuing or tracking animals with the intent to kill or trap something. Just as any animal has no chance of survival against a human equipped with a weapon; this is the case for you against the Gods. God Yahweh says he is love, and wants you to learn how to love one other on earth. But how can you obey these rules when he doesn't follow his own commandments. (KJV)-Deuteronomy 6:5 says; "Love the Lord your God with all your heart and with all your soul and with your entire mind." This is the first and greatest commandment. The second is from (KJV)-Matthew 22:39; "Love your neighbor as yourself." And the third is from (KJV)-Ephesians 2:10, as it says; "We are God's workmanship, created in Christ Jesus to do good works, which God prepared in advance for us to do." All of the loving Gods laws basically hang on these three commandments but God is an entity that cannot follow his own rules, but wants you too; here are the Ten Commandments that the loving God Yahweh has given you:

1. *You shall have no other gods before me*: I believe in learning from others mistakes. Egyptians, Romans, Christians, Germans, Catholics, Islams, Hinduism, Buddhism, Baptists, Protestants, Mormons, etc.; the list of religions are endless, have all been in communication with the loving God Yahweh before and after the born savior Christ arrived: and all have still sought after something greater, a replacement if you will. The problem is that God doesn't do anything for himself; he gets someone else to do his dirty work, and gets angry at humanity for getting it wrong; a very judgmental entity. An example, God sent a savior named Jesus Christ to save the world; because the universe kept on, kept on, and kept on sinning. Why didn't God do it himself; instead sending his son to do it for him. Jesus did not make this mess called life, but yet had to die a gruesome death on a cross. This loving God Yahweh is always asking for someone else to fix the problems that he makes.

2. *You shall not make idols.* Touching on the subject briefly in # 1, people have always made objects to worship. Idolatry connotes the worship of an object, something or someone other than God as if it were God. Human beings need something they can see and touch; still the living Gods remain invisible. All religions worship some sort of constructed material; the sun dial, burning candles, paintings, statues, money, artifacts, and animals, to name a few to fill a void. The loving God will not show himself to us; as no

one has ever physically seen him. God Yahweh is arrogant and never leaves his throne in heaven; especially not for you, you are not worth it.

3.  *You shall not take the name of the lord your God in vain.* Given the world that we live in, it is hard to not curse God. I have talked to many people regarding this subject, and the answer has always been the same; there are always more bad days than good. How can you love an entity that promises you a better world called 'heaven', when he did not get it right the first time, here on earth? God considers himself to be perfect, so why not get it right the first time. Who cares that the world is beautiful in nature; we never enjoy it like we should, with what; the busyness of our lives maintaining the greediness of a dollar to survive. The daily grind of waking up and working is a waste. All the majority of the world is doing is working to pay bills and thinking that they are getting ahead. We are dying, crying, and hurting down here. But you think that the loving God has a concern?

4.  *Remember the Sabbath day, to keep it holy.* Let me explain how we have this day incorrect and twisted from the start. If you want the truth, I guess read the bible for yourself. The bible says that God created the earth in six days and rested on the seventh. Look at our calendar, what is the first day of the week; it is Sunday! and the last; it is Saturday! Sunday through Friday is the six working days, and Saturday is our Sabbath day, the day of rest. But Sunday is the church going day across the globe. Please start reading and understanding what you are reading, you have it all wrong and are living in a world that has no clue what they are doing.

5.  *Honor your father and your mother.* Pretty straight forward, right? I don't know about that. Raising children has forever been a full

job in itself. From your children growing up from toddler = pre-teen = teenager = young adult = to adult, it is quite a journey. In the day and age that we live in today, there have never been more kids disrespecting their parents than ever before. I say that, but I was not around 2,000 years ago. Parents probably had it bad back then as well. And the effect of this, parents giving up on their child, missing out on keen moments in their lives, bad influential friends, stress over what to do next, or college entry exams, a future. How do you make peace with someone that you love, when you have no peace within yourself?

6. *You shall not murder.*

    1. Let's be truthful with one another, God Yahweh is a murderer. The simple fact that you are born, live a life, and die makes him a murderer. He gave your life, and takes it. You had no control over any of it. (KJV)-Ecclesiastes 3:18-19; you are no better than a dog.
    2. Nowhere in the bible does it say that you will go to hell if you commit suicide; but this has been taught in many religions. This issue has been a problem ever since the beginning. I have a section in this book even speaking of Adam, 'the first man', committing suicide because this world is worthless and difficult. Although it does not say anything in the bible; you have to use common sense, you are still committing murder, 'yourself', and you cannot ask for forgiveness after you are dead, so you are not in a good position.

7. *You shall not commit adultery.* This is cheating on your spouse or significant other. It is deeper than that. If you are shacking up and not married, this covers it as well, because you are not supposed to have pre-marital sex. As hard as that is, being married to one

woman and seeing all these sexy ladies walking around this earth; it is hard to stay faithful to your wife, forever! I am not making excuses for cheating; I just think in reality. I am not the one who gave you these rules. God is the one who tells us that we can have only one mate for our entire lifetime. Obviously, the world is not following this format. Again, God knew you could not follow this rule.

8. *You shall not steal.* Stealing is taking (another person's property) without permission or legal right and without intending to return it. God steals, but wants you not to do it. A thirty-year-old man who dies in a car crash or a 10 years old girl dying from leukemia; I would say they were robbed of their life: he stole a life ahead of schedule. She could have gone on to accomplish great things, or maybe not; the point is that she never had the chance. Yes, I know, the bible never says life is fair. That does not make a family member mourn the loss of a loved one any less. But why people steal can take many other forms; such as the thrill of getting away with it, to get even with someone, or out of necessity. As the person stealing is feeling happy and proud of what they have just done; the counterpart is sad and aggravated.

9. *You shall not bear false witness against your neighbor.* This is lying or lying on someone else for the benefit of your future. From the smallest white lie to an extensive black lie. Most everybody, at one time or another, has lied. Tell the truth now: that includes you and me. In fact, some people, sad to say, lie almost all the time. Psychologists call these people compulsive or psychopathic liars. They tell lies even when they do not have to. Even the

youngest of children will lie, especially if they think by doing it they will not be punished for something from their parent or teacher. When children first learn how lying works, they lack the moral understanding of when to refrain from doing it. If children cannot understand the difference, then what does it say about adults? Adults are supposed to be more mature, understanding, with a stable mind. Lying can have such destructive and harmful consequences to both the liar and the one being lied to; but still not enough of horrible repercussions, as we still lie.

10. *You shall not covet.* This particular command is telling you not to want what someone else has. It could be anything from material possessions to another person's spouse being more attractive than yours. This is pretty hard to do. God knows we have a selfish heart; and to ask such a thing is delusional. It is human nature to be self-centered; it was designed in our dna. 'Jealous' is defined as being very watchful with something we already possess (usually when a special relationship) is threatened by a third person; while 'Envy' is defined as a feeling of discontent and ill will because of another's advantages, possessions, etc.; resentful dislike of another who has something that one desires. The Biblical sin is called "envy," not "jealousy": When you "covet thy neighbor's wife," you are resentful that your neighbor has her, and you do not. How many a men have coveted a woman; and how many a woman, have coveted a man, that was not their spouse. Or a car or house that their neighbor has, because it is better. In this world of flashiness, it is difficult to be content.

- Can you love a God that gave you this world, it is pointless and worthless?
- Can you really love someone else, when the entity that created you does not love you?
- Can you really be happy for someone else when they have a better life than you?

# DAY 9: STAGE 9

Your life on this earth does not matter to God, not one bit.

In the book of (KJV)-Jeremiah 29:11, the loving God says; "For I know the plans I have for you, 'declares the Lord', plans to prosper you and not to harm you, plans to give you hope and a future". My question to you is; are you prospering; are you happy and enjoying moments living on this planet; are you really satisfied? Alternatively, you work 40+ hours a week and still have bills stacked to the ceiling and cannot see the light at the end of the tunnel? Thoughts of a husband cheating or wife? Thoughts about how to pay taxes? Thoughts of your life being cut short by a murder or accident? See the loving God Yahweh tells you the great and wonderful things that you want to hear, but the conditions that you see and experience in your individual lives tell otherwise. Stop thinking in simple manners: Just because you have a lot does not mean it will provide what you need; more is less and less is more, understand.

Why were you a male born 5'-9" tall, instead of 6'-2", with no athleticism? Automatically, your dreams are minimized. You do not have the chance to play in professional sports making millions of dollars a year; while another is blessed with athletic on top of athletic capabilities. Or why are you not as smart as someone else; unable to come up with an invention to change the world as another can, helpless to make your life as successful as you'd like it to be; working a dead end job? Blame the God who promises to make it all better.

Women; you are so beautiful, amazing, and special, but asked to bear the weight of the world on your shoulders. You do not receive the praise you deserve. Without you, the world would come to a screeching halt. You bear children, raise them, some of these children becoming men, and you are not treated equally in the workplace in regards to pay, position, assignments, and advancements as men occupy; when you are just as qualified. Women's professional sports do not pay nearly as much as men do, so some sort of office job is your future, where you face sexual harassment as another pain in your side. Blame the God who promises to make it all better. The situations that you are placed in; a simple man has no idea the burden you carry. There are two types of discrimination in the workforce, as only 42% of women have reported it:

- *Statistical discrimination;* which is rooted in beliefs about average gender differences in abilities or skills; results when economic agents (consumers, employers, etc.) have imperfect information about individuals they interact with.
- *Taste-based discrimination;* which is driven by stereotypes, favoritism for one group, and a bias against another group; and argues that employers experience negative effects because of hiring a particular group of workers, such as women.

The loving God claims that he wants you to know the truth about this life as (KJV)-John 8:32 says; "Then you will know the truth, and the truth shall set you free." Then (KJV)- Ecclesiastes 8:17 saying; "I saw every work of God, and that a man is unable to comprehend the work that is done under the sun. Despite his efforts to search it out, he cannot find its meaning; even if the wise man claims to know, he is unable to comprehend." God Yahweh is a contradictory God; the two verses just mentioned tell us the opposite feelings. The truth is your reality.

Since the beginning of creation, man and woman have been begging and crying to the heavens for the loving God to rescue them from a dreadful life we live, but he turns a deaf ear on you. The bible is clear that the two sins which cannot be forgiven is blasphemy against the Holy Spirit, and the refusal to believe in Jesus Christ. (KJV)-Mark 3:29; "But whoever blasphemes against the Holy Spirit will never be forgiven, he is guilty of an eternal sin." (KJV)- Mark 16:16; "Whoever believes and is baptized will be saved but whoever does not believe will be condemned."

These Gods want you to go through these trials and tribulations in your life because they hate you; both of them. You expect the one that hates you to despise you (Satan); but never in a million years did you anticipate the one claiming to love you, instead loathing you (Yahweh). You have always wondered why life is hard, and the way it is, well, there you have it, the truth. There is no life to discover except the one that is staring you right in the face: your reality. The best use of your life is to use it on yourself; no one else helps you, so why should you help anyone else. You have tried to help others, and what happens? They take advantage of you or hurt you in the process; countess times over and over again. Even to the point where you want to help someone, but step back because you know what will happen. You are sick and tired of being hurt and emotionally vulnerable.

God says that relationships are the key to life. Do you believe this? If relationships were so important, why did he make the world with so much confrontation? Your weekdays are so busy; you do not have time to spend with your family at night. Weekends are filled with errands, catching up on work, etc. Here are five sayings about what God does for you, and have become very popular among church go-ers, believers, and non-believers to help themselves get through tough times.

1.  *God won't give you more than you can handle*.
    (KJV)-1 Corinthians 10:13 says; "There hath no temptation taken hold of you but such as is common to man. But God is faithful; He will not suffer you to be tempted beyond that which ye are able to bear, but with the temptation will also make a way to escape, that ye may be able to bear it." When a difficulty arises in the life a believer (or anyone else), this supposed verse is tossed out there like a Scripture bomb. Sure, it sounds compelling, and is supposed to remind us of God's care and concern for each of us.

    How true is this, you be the judge? You always try your best and when you get one-step ahead in your life, something occurs, and you fall back three steps. So no, he does give you more than you can handle. There are times in your life when you feel like throwing in the towel. And many people have. When God says he never gives you more than you can handle; that is a bold-faced lie. He does give you more than you can handle, and you know it. He gives you more than you can handle so you can realize that you cannot handle it on your own and depend on him, and rid us of our pride. This is a psychotic manner in handing things. (KJV)- Proverbs 16:18 says; "Pride goes before destruction, a haughty spirit before a fall." To keep us grounded in the reality of our need for a Savior, God graciously allows us to see just how much we cannot handle. He tasked the eleven apostles with spreading the gospel all over the world, but all have died a gruesome death in the process. Why do I not mention the twelfth one you ask; because he sold out Jesus Christ to God Satan and died ahead of his time. Nevertheless, all of these apostles had their life ended by having their heads chopped off, burned alive, fed to animals, or locked in a dungeon until his last breath. Again, here is your loving God Yahweh at his best.

2. *If God brings you to it, He will lead you through it.*

This verse does conjure up images of the Israelites passing through the Red Sea or Joshua leading God's people through the Jordan River. However, this is not necessarily what the Bible teaches. It is not true that God is with us always, no matter what we face. In (KJV)-Matthew 28; 20, Jesus says; "And surely I am with you always, to the very end of the age." Two reasons why this is false. One, Jesus will be there to the end of the age, and he will be the one to send you to hell if your name is not written in the book of life. So the fact is that he will not be with you for all of eternity. And two, God does not always remove us from a bad situation, sometimes he makes it worse. A struggling marriage, back irs payments, you end up getting a divorce even if neither one wants it, because you don't know how to communicate, or fall deeper into dept. You may never get "through" your struggle; this is something that you have to come to grips with. God may lead you to stay right where you are so that you can have an impact there-and he can get the glory; his selfish reasons.

3. *If God closes one door, He'll open another (or a giant window).*

You could say this folklore verse is closely associated with number two above. It has the same potential for stock image inspiration in your social media feed, and has no truth to it. The bible does not promise that God will keep us headed in the right direction; (KJV)-Psalms 32:8 says; "I will instruct you and teach you in the way you should go, I will counsel you and watch over you." But the "way you should go" doesn't necessarily mean God will plan an escape hatch for you when times get tough or when you don't seem to be making progress. Human beings tend to want to go in their own direction, so if the loving God is saying something to them, they ignore it, and do not even hear it, and he lets go of you. But after being burned multiple times in life, who wants to trust any longer? The definition of trust is firm belief in the reliability, truth, ability, or strength of someone or something. (KJV)-Psalm 37:7 says; "Be still before the LORD and wait patiently for him; do not fret when men succeed in their ways, when they carry out their wicked schemes." If God stops something good from happening in your life, immediately look for another way through and direction. He is not in it to help you; he is in it to help himself.

4. *Your wish is my command,' says the Lord.*

Okay, so this is not a verse, but some people in the world like to treat God like a Jeanie in a bottle, and the sentiment has certainly been shared all over the globe. If you keep asking; if you believe enough; if you have faith enough, then God will give you whatever you want. (KJV)- Psalm 37:4 says to; "Delight yourself in the LORD and he will give you the desires of your heart." The hot blond with big breasts that a man desires so badly, is she going to flock to you if you don't look like Brad Pitt; I think not. The high paying job that you need, never going to happen unless you feed the system of colleges and universities; and then still not a guarantee. The loving God teases you, showing you things you want and need, but can never have.

I know you have tried the loving God in your life, and have ended up disappointed. You cannot count on all your fingers and toes how many times you have been disheartened in your life. So, does God answer our prayers? Maybe. Should you bring your needs to him? Maybe. But I cannot trust it. Should we expect Him to answer our prayers exactly as we want? No—not unless we are mainly praying and desiring for HIS will to be done. We are a self-centered race, of course, we do not want his will, and we want OURS!

5. *God loves you and has a wonderful plan for your life!*

Many, many years ago, this phrase became a staple of evangelism, and since then, it has taken on an aura of something biblical. The problem though, is that it suggests an idea that is not biblical at all. How? Let us break it down in (KJV)-Romans 5:8. The problem is that God never says he loved YOU, God said he loved the WORLD, (KJV)-John 3:16 says; "For God so loved the world, that he gave his only begotten Son, that whosoever believeth in him shall not perish, but have everlasting life." He never said I love you; to you personally, the world and you are two separate items. God loved the world that he created, not you.

Nevertheless, the trouble starts when we add to that the idea that once we are saved, everything will suddenly be awesome. Despite what it may have meant at one time, that "wonderful plan for your life" part sounds an awful lot like "He'll fix all your problems." The truth is that following Jesus may actually cause more problems for the believer. Jeremiah obeyed God's call, and he ended up at the bottom of a cistern. David trusted God, and he spent years running for his life and dodging spears. Paul surrendered to Christ, and he forfeited prestige for prison.

## **Proactive versus Reactive**

Being proactive describes a situation where you attempt to prevent a controversy before it takes place; reactive is where you respond to the situation after the fact. The loving God Yahweh is a reactive entity. First, God knew what Lucifer would eventually become: and that was Satan, a prideful, resentful, and despicable entity, but so is God Yahweh. Instead of letting us have peace and harmony in our world, God lets us have the world we know now, and 'then' offers redemption in the form of Jesus Christ. But what is happening to you in the meantime? He drags you through the mud, experiencing unbearable pain that comes along with this life.

Second, the supposedly loving God Yahweh wanted you to hurt in this world, and he is the author of sin. How can you not be the author when everything has been preordained, in other words, his will? We are nothing but puppets in his scheme of things. He knew Satan would tempt, and Adam would fall. (KJV)-Psalm 139:1-6 says; "Lord, you have examined me and know all about me. You know when I sit down and when I get up. You know my thoughts before I think them. You know where I go and where I lie down. You know everything I do. Lord, even before I say a word, you already know it. You are all around me—in front and in back—and have put your hand on me. Your knowledge is amazing to me; it is more than I can understand." God knew how all this would happen and wanted it to happen. He did not do anything to prevent it. The sin that began in the Garden of Eden served as the basis for which human sin entered the world, our constant suffering and pain, and thus needing to reveal the necessity of the one who could conquer sin and death, this being Jesus Christ. (KJV)-Romans 8:2 teaches; "For the law of the Spirit of life has set you free in Christ Jesus from the law of sin and death." But his plan has backfired. Because I believe that he has mis-judged our human nature. (KJV)-Matthew 7:13-14 says; That few will enter heaven and many will be in hell. Who wants to be with someone that makes them to go through hardships and agony, is deceptive, and punishes, when it could all have been avoided.

Third, God created humans with freedom of choice, 'free will'. The only other alternatives were to create people without choice or to not make people at all. People without choice would create a robotic type of existence that does not reflect the plan of God for the world. Instead, God created people with the ability to make choices, including right and wrong, as part of His sovereign creation. Ultimately, we have become automated to some extent, you wake up at a certain time every morning and leave work every evening at a certain time.

Don't you feel like a robot anyway?

# DAY 10: STAGE 10

Have you read the entire bible, more importantly; did you fully comprehend it?

(KJV)-Acts 1 7:8 tells us; "It is not for you to know times or seasons that the Father has fixed by his own authority. But you will receive power when the Holy Spirit has come upon you, and you will be my witness in Jerusalem and in all Judea and Samaria, and to the end of the earth." Both Gods are filthy disgusting entities; as there is a ton of very disturbing stories throughout the bible. I won't disclose all of them, but I will give you a few of some abominable things the good God says to us; and I would prefer for you to really read and understand these so called entities that created you. The evil God has a book as well, most communities do not want to converse on this book, but it is out there; called 'The Satanic bible'. More importantly, the overwhelming theme is that the good God is also an evil devil; we expect the loving God to be pleasing, but he is not, as these seven scriptures listed below, came from the bible. You are a virus!

1. Moloch; a demon, found in the old testament:

Take my word at its face value; societies and families are still practicing these rituals today, as they have done for all of time. The information that I am presenting to you, is actual, and not a stunt. In (KJV)-Jeremiah 32:35, it talks of an entity named Moloch, saying; "They

Never, never was trustworthy?

built the high places of Baal in the valley of the son of Hinnom, to offer up their sons and daughters to Moloch, though I did not command them, nor did it enter into my mind, that they should do this abomination, to cause Judah to sin." who is this, and how important is this Moloch, for him to be mentioned in the Christian bible to begin with? (KJV)-Leviticus 18:21 also says; "You shall not give your children to offer them to Moloch, and so profane the name of your God: I am the lord." Moloch was a Canaanite God, who I really believe to be a powerful demon that people sacrificed their children to, for worldly gain, profit or to achieve a desired result. This is not uncommon, as even the good, loving God; sacrificed his own son, commanding him to become a man, and die a horrible death, to satisfy the sins of humanity. If you are a great and almighty God, why do you need human sacrifice; it seems belittling. This is not love, it is bloodshed. I think the good God became jealous; as people began to sacrifice their children to Moloch; instead of the good God. The innocent children that go missing on the back of milk cartons, or on your police stations missing youth boards; unfortunately, never get found. And the reason for this is that they are sacrificed. Who is doing the sacrificing? Your governments, hollywood, military, the music industry, and plain people walking out and about in broad daylight seeking to have a better life.

2.  The Book of Enoch:

There is a book that was left out of the Christian bible called "The book of Enoch"! If you can come across it, it will blow your mind, and let you know that this was really all; just an experiment to the Gods. This story was the reason why "The flood of Noah" took place. During the days of Noah, women were stunning, absolutely gorgeous; but the world was a mess, as it is today; sound familiar? Anyway, there were a group of angels in heaven, probably thousands; called 'The Watchers', who were supposed to keep an eye on humans, and keep the noble ones from trouble. What happened next; is that the angels saw that the women were so beautiful and from Pseudepiprapha, Enoch 6:2 tells us; "And the angels, the children of heaven, saw them and desired them; and they said to one another, "Come, let us choose wives for ourselves from among the daughters of man and beget us children." Then in Enoch 7:1; "And they took wives unto themselves, and everyone respectively chose one woman for himself, and they began to go unto them. And they taught them magical medicine, incantations, the cutting of roots, and taught them about plants." What this is saying, is that angels took human form and had intercourse with women. The angels being able to transform themselves into handsome men, had no problem attracting women. The result of this; these women gave birth to gigantic children, some as tall as 16 feet tall. They were called 'Nephilim': the offspring of 'the sons of the loving God', and 'the daughters of men'. These beings started to eat men and children and were terrifying. What a good God who is control of everything; letting things like this happen.

3.   <u>God answers to himself alone.</u>

(KJV)-Psalm 135:6 tells us that; "The lord does whatever pleases him, in the heavens and on the earth, in the seas and all their depths." I see this as you obtaining as much satisfaction on the earth as possible, and enjoying your life as you see fit, because you only live once, and the Gods are going to send you wherever they want, heaven or hell. I do not see the point in creating us, if you are going to control things, and be a tyrant. If you believe in serving a good God, you are also serving an egotistical and narcissistic God. They are one in the same, except one pretends to be good, and the other evil, play the game as well. The evil god definitely hates you, but the so-called good God does not give a damn about you as well; they do not need you, they don't need me, they don't need any of this.

4. <u>God creates people have deformities, but doesn't care to have them around him.</u>

This verse tells you we are dealing with two Gods and not one all mighty creator. (KJV)- Leviticus 21:17-23 tells us; "Say to Aaron: For the generations to come, none of your descendants who has a defect may come near to offer the food of his God. No man who has any defect may come near: no man who is blind or lame, disfigured or deformed; no man with a crippled foot or hand, or who is hunchbacked or dwarfed, or who has an eye defect, or who has festering or running sores or damaged testicles. No descendant of Aaron the priest who has any defect is to come near to present the offerings made to the lord by fire. If he has a defect; he must not come near to offer the food of his God. He may eat the most holy food of his God, as well as the holy food; yet because of his defect, he must not go near the curtain or approach the altar, and so desecrate my sanctuary. I am the lord, who makes them holy." Yes, people reading this, this is your good God Yahweh; who created you, telling you to stay away if you have a defect, which will desecrate his sanctuary. The thing that gets me about such verses is how people knew who could go in to worship God and who couldn't. Make no mistake about it, these rules still apply to our modern age. (KJV)-Deuteronomy 23:1 says; "He who is emasculated by crushing or mutilation shall not enter the assembly of the lord." I am being sarcastic; yeah, the good God loves us. Not. <u>Desecrate definition</u>: treat a sacred place or thing with violent disrespect; violate.

5.  Sex slavery condoned.

In our modern day, young girls, escorts and prostitutes are more available than ever before. The sex and trade industry of young girls are the ones that hurt me the most; under the age of 12, but it does not seem to hurt the good and loving God. But who can blame us for what we do; your God has been allowing this to happen endlessly. (KJV)-Exodus 21:7-8 says; "If a man sells his daughter as a servant, she is not to go free as male servants do. If she does not please the master who has selected her for himself, he must let her be redeemed. He has no right to sell her to foreigners, because he has broken faith with her." The sex trade in the world is abundant. Parents care more about money in a second and third world country, and apparently in a first world country as well, than their children. Look, I did not write the bible, I am just telling you the truth. It hurts my heart every day, to think of a 40-year-old man having sex with a 12-year-old, but this is your God allowing it to happen. My personal experience: when I was 22 years of age, I met a woman in Lafayette, LA. Her age at the time of our meeting was 34, and we developed a positive relationship between us, she confided in me one day, telling me that her mother sold her at the age of sixteen, to a man that was forty-two. Believe me, it happens more than you think. She divorced the person as soon as she turned eighteen. But what a horrible incident.

6.  Cannibalism.

(KJV)-2 Kings 6:28-29 tells us about a story when it said; "She answered, this woman said to me, 'Give up your son so we may eat him today, and tomorrow we'll eat my son.' So we cooked my son and ate him. The next day I said to her, 'Give up your son so we may eat him', but she had hidden him." What in the world is this? This occurred during a famine in the city of Samaria. Based on our financial structure today, a lot of people go without food. Many children in America, let alone the world; only sources of food are during lunch at school. I am not saying that parents will eat their children, but we are not headed in the best direction. Our land for crops are steadily being minimized, due to the industrial, and construction era; furthermore, reducing number of harvests, and leading the way for the production of more genetically modified foods.

7.  The Throne in Heaven, The Throne in Hell.

The good God sits on the throne, and (KJV)-Revelation 4:4-7 speaks of; "Surrounding the throne were twenty-four other thrones, and seated on them were twenty-four elders. They were dressed in white and had crowns of gold on their heads. From the throne came flashes of lighting, rumblings, and peals of thunder. Before the throne, seven lamps were blazing. These were the seven spirits of the good God. Also, before the throne there was what looked like a sea of glass, clear as crystal. In the center, around the throne, were four living creatures, and they were covered with eyes, in front and in back. The first living creature was like a lion, the second like an ox, the third had a face like a man, the fourth was like a flying eagle." This is the weird idiocy that we are dealing with here. First of all, the twenty-four elders are supposed to be people, people that were so good on earth, that the good God consults them for advice; I have no idea who they are, you guess is as good as mine. What in the world is these other 4 creatures?

Those seven examples listed above, upon many others came from the mouth of your loving God Yahweh. But do not worry, the other is just as awful, as they are copy cats of each other; Satan has his throne in hell, with his twenty-four elders of evil persons from the earth. He has seven spirits as well, with his army of demons by his side. (KJV)-Revelation 12:3-4; "Then another sign appeared in heaven: an enormous red dragon with seven heads and then horns and seven crowns on his heads. His tail swept a third of the stars out of the sky and flung them to the earth. The dragon stood in front of the woman who was about to give birth, so that he might devour her child the moment it was born." other verses in (KJV)-Revelation 13:1-2 and (KJV)-Revelation 13:11.

This type of substance is a lot to take in; as these Gods are not from our world, have no idea what it is like to be a human, yet give us ridiculous rules to follow, setting you up for failure, and damning you to hell. And it will not change, as (KJV)-Malachi 3:6 says; "For I the Lord do not change; therefore, you, O children of Jacob, are not consumed." I challenge you to really read what is being said in this book called the bible, comprehend it and see what kind of preposterous items are said in here, supposedly all coming from a loving and caring God Yahweh.

What shall we do?

# DAY 11: STAGE 11

You were the God's slaves before you were the world's slaves.

Bondage:   1. Slavery or involuntary servitude; serfdom.
2. The state of being bounded by or subjected to some external power or control.
3. The state or practice of being physically restrained, as by being tied up, chained, or put in handcuffs, for sexual gratification.

I will give you the key to your happiness and contentment. Take it, and enjoy the rest of your drive. In addition, I will not charge you; the key to happiness/ joy and contentment/fulfillment is putting you 'first'; what you care, believe and think about in yourself, and never about what another being thinks of you or this life, not even the Gods, because you only get one go around on this planet. You cannot love someone else: until you first learn to love yourself. Even the God that created us did not get this right. What others think and believe has never mattered and it never will, no one else in the world matters accept you; in a hundred years, the society you view today, will not be around; everyone will be in the dirt or cremated somewhere far off and not exist any longer. Nevertheless, for some reason and I could never understand why; we have always given emphasis and concern on what others think. The only person you can control is yourself; body and mind.

Forget about pleasing the Gods, it is a task that simply cannot be done; he gave a worthless book to read from called the bible, that will stand the test of time; situations that applied three thousand years ago still do today, and will three thousand more. Pleasing the Gods is a battle that cannot be won. You have to look within yourself, and I know you say this is hard; it is really not. The moment you start to make yourself joyful, you will be greater. I am not talking about material things and sexual pleasures. I realize those are the items you so desperately desire, but you can have five cars, ten bedrooms, three girlfriends, how many can you use at one time? That is your bondage and you never knew it before, you want so much, but can only enjoy one detail at a time.

There is a peace inside your soul, but most, almost everyone, does not know how to access this powerful concept, because we are ripping and running around making money, pleasing our spouse and kids, amusing our parents, charming our bosses, obtaining the next piece of technology that will never fill that void in your situational life. Be satisfied with who you are; you cannot be anyone else but you, and cannot enjoy anyone else but you. You cannot look like anyone else but you, and do not have the gifts and endowment that others have. Trust me, when I say, that another can have all the physical and intellectual favor of the world, but inside, are never satisfied.

*This planet called Earth:*

This whole world is a form of bondage, every inch of it, if you have not figured this out for yourself: we were never meant to ever leave this planet. We sometimes say the world is a big place; but it is not. It is very small actually. We cannot travel anywhere else but where we are now, so you are bonded and limited by space. There is a large galaxy out there, which we will never have the chance to experience; we claim we can go to Mars or Jupiter, but that is an irrational statement. Yes, I give technology some credit, but not that much. When I was a kid, I heard stories about flying cars, cities in the sky, going to Pluto as plans for the future. We are not even remotely close to accomplishing these ambitions. Robots and machinery can do it, as they do not have to worry about breathing, amongst other issues we possess. This will hit closer to home; you have a quarrel with someone and hope to never see them ever again, then 20 years later, your paths cross again in the most inopportune place. What do you do? How do you react?

You are in bondage by time and space.

1. *Money and Finances:*

If you take a lighter to a hundred-dollar bill and burn it, what is it worth; absolutely nothing. We believe that the more money you have offers higher levels of freedom, which it does to some extent, but whether you are ashamed or too proud to admit it; no it really does not. More money brings bigger problems and demands, and makes you less happy and more worried; weird how this works out. I do not care if you are a millionaire, billionaire, or trillionaire, I do not need to know who you are or meet you, and I can guarantee that your life is sad, lonely, and you are a lost soul. (KJV)-Mark 8:36 says; "For whoever wants to save his life will lose it, but whoever loses his life for my sake and for the gospel will save it. What does it profit a man to gain the whole world, yet forfeit his soul? Or what can a man give in exchange for his soul?" I am not the most environmental aware person, but I do know that we have gone past the point of no return; that even if we stopped the industrial industry today, it is already too late. We have destroyed our world behind money and greed. You are in bondage of money.

2. *Work and Status:*

Work can be in the same category as money, but it is different. Work: can be defined as the exchanging of time and energy for a profitable gain. Money is our primary exchange, now, but it was animals, clothing, food and water, human necessities, before the invention of currency. Depending on how much you make, is it worth it? Now I know, that it is necessary to make money to live and provide, but it is not worth all the trouble if you really think about it. You are forced to put your head down and work for forty years, and then one day you look in the mirror, and you have aged, and what have you obtained? Did you enjoy those forty years? Or did you work so hard that you can barely walk and take care of yourself in your old age? Have you missed out on beautiful moments with your family and friends?

You are in bondage to the clock at work.

3. *Marriage:*

I know some people will get a kick out of this next subject; especially women. The man was put in charge; and the woman was designed to submit in the relationship. KJV)-Ephesians 5:22 tells us; "Wives, submit yourselves to your own husbands as you do to the Lord." Also, (KJV)-Ephesians 5:25 says; "Husbands, love your wives, just as Christ loved the church and gave Himself up for her." We are a far cry from these commands, as the divorce rate for the world is between 60%-75%. My father will probably be upset by telling this story, but knowing him, I do not think he will be; but I have to examine this situation. When my parents earned the sanctity of marriage, there is a picture of them walking out of the church. When seeing my father's face, he looked like the most jubilant man in the world, but in regards to my mother, her glance was one that resembled panic. They have been married for forty-two years as I write this, and he has confessed to me that it has been pure difficulty and unrest during the course of these years. They should have divorced twenty-two years ago, but have not, and being unhappy in a relationship is not a good state. Men try to be in charge while women try to control. You are always fighting against the grain in your rapport. What causes a happy and pleasant relationship to become sour and bitter? Is it your fault, your spouse, both? You do not ask the right questions to fix your problems. This can even occur in homosexuality affairs; as there is a male and female representative in either a Lesbian or Gay association.

- In Charge: in control or with overall responsibility of someone or something.
- In Control: the power to influence or direct people's behavior or the course of events.

4. *Prayer:*

Do you consider this a form of bondage; well, you should. Bondage is also defined as holding something over the head against another. This is what the good God does with prayer, and situations have been noted about making pacts/deals with Satan. If your friend asks for something from you, and you do not give it to him or her unless they say please and thank you; that is a form of bondage. You are withholding something they need and demanding something in return before handing over the prize. That is prayer. God Yahweh supposedly knows all your wants and needs; but doesn't give it to you until you pray to him, and more often than not, you still do not receive what you are asking for. It is sorrowful that God does not give us what we need to begin with. If you want to know, why you were placed on this planet, you must begin with you. You were born by the Gods to be their slaves, and we have decided that we want to do our own motives, as is the reason for the distress of the world.

5. *Drugs, Alcohol, Smoking, Gambling, and other substance abusers:*

People see it as a temporary situation because they are in physical pain or because they are dealing with grief or loss. Recognizing there is a problem is the first step to dealing with a dependence or addiction. This is your loving and good God; providing a life that is so hard that people need dependencies to get through a day, a week, a month, a year, etc. if your life is not stressful enough, the use of these items can add to more serious problems including anything from altered brain chemistry, health complications, infections, legal issues, financial problems, accidental injuries, and even death. The percentage of you not being with the good God is greater than being with him. Since we never seem to please him, never satisfy him, how can we expect to make it to heaven, nothing we do is good enough. By a person, named Jesus Christ and a concept called faith. Faith is complete trust or confidence in someone or something in the unseen world. You have to make your own decision, but I cannot trust the unseen; especially when I see reality every day and night, when I walk out the front door. These Gods do not even show themselves to us; how can you believe in a great future, when the present has always been a disaster. (KJV)-Proverbs 20:1 says; "Wine is a mocker, strong drink a brawler, and whoever is led astray by it is not wise."

What is wrong with the world is the fact that we have gods. If the gods would have just let you do your own thing, you probably would be a decent human being. The fact that they intervene and you never knew it. The rich, poor or middle class is not ruining life. Yahweh wants it a certain way and Satan wants it a particular way and they intervene in your life. The idea of free will is an illusion discussed in depth in stage nineteen. Clearly, it is on your and the stranger's mind in a big way at some point today, and it made me think: is that what I write about here? What is wrong with the world? Sometimes, I guess. Did they find what they were looking for, I wonder.

When people ask what's wrong with the world, it's usually in response to some human-caused tragedy so I think it's safe to say they mean the human world. I don't think they're referring to the planet itself, its fault lines or geographic blemishes. It's not usually an earnest question either, it's an exclamation expressed as a rhetorical question, like "Why the hell would anyone eat pink licorice?" And you know, I'm not sure I've ever treated it as a face-value question. I certainly never articulated an answer. Women-do you hate God for letting you be fucked, instead of doing the fucking. Men-do you hate God for not giving you the pretty lady, instead of an ugly lady. Because deep down in your soul, he implanted these feelings. I am not talking about the simple answers of he is crazy/has no sense. She should have waited till she was married to have a child. He should not have done drugs. She should have gone to school. Religion has failed; yet religion was never the problem nor the good or lack of an economy.

Stop being a simpleton and think larger.

I am not here to hurt you; but to give you the truth.

# DAY 12: STAGE 12

The spirit of religion is precarious and damn right malicious, both sides, 'good and evil'.

Religious denomination divides you as a people, you know this; yet you still participate in it. The God's created you for their own selfish reasons. They never showed any concern or asked how hungry you would become, how your body aches, how your spouse beats on you, and how lonely you would be here. I am sure that while growing up as a child, if you were fortunate or unfortunate to go to church every Sunday morning with your parents, family or friends, you basically sat there in the pew bored out of your mind, wondering what the hell am I doing here, listening to this person talk about the good God being so great, disagreeing all the while, keeping your thoughts to yourself. <u>Religion</u> is defined as the belief and worship of a supreme being or controlling power; for the benefit of personal worldly status. Be honest, what do you pray to your God for? Every now and then, you pray for good health, another person, or a family member, but mostly; you pray for more money, winning the lottery, a better job, a new mate, your favorite team to win, someone to be fired so you can live a better worldly life and be fabulous. You want to purchase as many material items as you can. You want clothes, cars, houses, jewelry, popularity, etc. Why do you desire these things so badly; is it because your soul is barren, lonely, and desperate for attention?

Why do you keep going back and forth with your God; I am glad you asked me that question. For a period of a person's life, they love God; then another period, they hate him, this is not the makings of a stable relationship. You do not know what to think or welcome. The issue for me is; we have an alleged perfect being creating imperfect people, generation after generation, and wants to judge you for your errors and sins. Your almighty good God has much hate in his heart for you, treating you like a dog who never obeys. In our society, it is considered important to respect other people's points of view even if you do not share their beliefs, especially where religion is concerned, because it is a subject people feel very strongly about. If the world found out that the Gods hated them, it would result in more chaos, anarchy, and disorder in our world. Knowing that God loves you, keeps you going, keeps you motivated, and keeps you focused. But I am sorry to tell you, my friends, that the Gods do not love you. So let the chaos begin or continue. As I am revealing the real truth to you, now you can find something else to do with your moments and efforts. Nevertheless, the forever issue is, people living their lives, being corrupt, sinful, evil, and doing whatever the hell they want, and think that the good God will let them into heaven on their death bed during the last seconds. It does not work like that my friend. If you believed you would spend a whole lifetime of doing naughty, mischievous, fraudulent things and then be forgiven at the drop of a dime, you are mistaken. I do not need to be a priest, pastor, deacon, or have a degree from a formal bible study seminar school to know what I am talking about; and neither do you. What do I always say, do the research and study for yourself and all will be given to you.

The subject of religion has mainly been used, as a controlling mechanism. So can institutions like governments, schools, marriage, and the military, but this chapter is strictly on religion. You see, human beings have always needed something to believe in. I have never seen God in person, have you? But the mind drifts into places that are not safe sometimes. You would go into a panic or shock knowing that you just evolved out of thin air, with questions of how, why, and when, and there was no God? Please do not go into dismay, the Gods do exist, they put you here on this earth, but they are not who you think they are! Moreover, we do have something to believe in, because we did not appear out nowhere. Unfortunately, organizations have taken advantage of the Gods: financially and emotionally, from the need for people to believe in something. In the book of revelation in the bible, seven churches are mentioned; and it is not the location of these churches that are of importance; but the spirits that they represent. You can go to any modern day church, or past chapels in the world, and these seven spirits will be active; guaranteed. These were the first seven churches to exist in the spirit of religion.

## These churches and spirits are as followed:

Philadelphia; old church in Revelation = a faithful church = spirit of inferiority = This church stayed steadfast in faith, that had kept God Yahweh's word and endured patiently. (The Christian Church is the modern day version of the church of Philadelphia.)

Smyrna; old church in Revelation = a persecuted church = spirit of oppression = This church was admired for its tribulation and poverty; forecasted to suffer persecution. (The Judaism Church is the modern day version of the church of Smyrna.)

Pergamum; old church in Revelation = a compromising church = spirit of bargain = This is the Church were God Satan's throne is; needed to repent of allowing false teachers. (The Islamic Church is modern day version of the church of Pergamum.)

Sardis; old church in Revelation = a dead church = spirit of traditionalism = This church is the church that has a good name; cautioned to fortify itself and return to God through repentance. (The Catholic Church is the modern day version of church of Sardis.)

Ephesus; old church in Revelation = a loveless church = spirit of religion = This church is known for having labored hard and not fainting, and separating themselves from the wicked; admonished for having forsaken its first love. (The Hinduism Church is the modern day version of the church of Ephesus.)

Thyatira; old church in Revelation = a corrupt church = spirit of control = This church is known for its charity, whose latter works are greater than the former, held the teachings of a false prophetess. (The Church of Scientology is the modern day version of the church of Thyatira.)

Laodicea; old church in Revelation = a lukewarm church = spirit of pride = This Church is lukewarm and insipid to God. (The Non-Denominational Church is the modern day version of the church of Laodicea.)

The book of (KJV)-James 1:26-27 says; "If anyone thinks he is religious and does not bridle his tongue but deceives his heart, this person's religion is worthless. Religion that is pure and undefiled before God, the father, is this; to visit orphans and widows in their affliction, and to keep oneself unstained from the world." When you go to church, pay attention to your pastors and congregation; to see who possesses these characteristics from the seven churches; it may even be you. One reason why the good God hates religion is because you are so busy judging what someone else is doing, while not paying attention to what you're participating in. You smile in another's face, but then curse and talk bad about them when they are gone. (KJV)- Matthew 7:3-5 says; "Why do you look at the speck of sawdust in your brother's eye and pay no attention to the plank in your own eye? How can you say to your brother, 'Let me take the speck out of your eye,' when all the time there is a plank in your own eye? You hypocrite, first take the plank out of your own eye, and then you will see clearly to remove the speck from your brother's eye." Every last church is full of hypocrites. Most people follow a religion because it is what their parents and grandparents did. This is called traditionalism.

All religions have flaws, not a single one is perfect, as they claim to be. Priests, pastors, clergymen, and elders are all looked at as if they can do no wrong, by the position they hold. Status and position were given just as fast as they can fail. The Catholic's molest each other and children; pay attention to the vatican, all these cardinals and priests have sexual encounters with one other. Islamic members kill people and each other to get to heaven. Christians think they are perfect, criticizing others; while they are far worse off than most. Mormons have more than one wife. Baptists believe once saved, always saved; which is not the case at all. Atheists do not believe in a God; and Agnostic's cannot make up their mind, he exists, he does not exist, I need more proof to make my decision. The history of religion refers to the written record of human religious' experiences and ideas. Organized religion is set out to make the other look bad, is this love: gossiping, pride, lies, envy all take place in the church: are these feelings of someone who love God? All add to the words that are in the bible, to make it more pleasant for their desires and cravings. If you can recall, I stick strictly to what is said in the scriptures.

The evil God, the devil; Satan, is definitely winning the war. During any course of history, society has always preferred to sin rather than obey commandments. How can the loving, good God Yahweh ever think that this could work? When it is all over and done with, there will definitely be more people in hell than in heaven. So again, I ask, what was the point of all this, if everyone was not going to make it to heaven. Why don't you ponder on that for a moment. 3/4 of the world's population at any given time will be experiencing anguish, discomfort, hardship, misery, torment, affliction, and distress for eternity in a place called hell; for what, 50-80 years' worth of life on this earth. Does anyone else see this as a raw deal? Yes, it is a raw deal, but what can we do? The wicked prospers in this world; and good people hurt and struggle in unimaginable ways. God keeps promising us a better life, a better situation, if we trust him and obey his commandments; but it never comes through; I know where you are, because I was there at one time. Everyone bickers and fights about what is right and what is wrong. I have given up on this. I am just living my life out until I die. It is pointless.

If I were the good God Yahweh, I would not care about this creation and you anymore either. I am writing this as George Herbert Walker Bush died on the week of November 30, 2018-December 7, 2019. Jesus Christ did not receive the amount of people showing up for his death, as he died for your sins; as Bush did, a simple, transparent man. You would rather show praise to a plain man instead of to the savior when he comes. 6,000 years later, religion is still a key player, as citizens of the earth will go to war and kill in the name of religion. They are prepared to fight for something they do not even know to be the truth. Don't we have loving Gods; Gods that let their prized possession, 'the creation', kill one another over them. I live life with no religion, but I do not need to belong to something to feel liked or welcomed. I am still and always will be a nice and descent person; because I chose to be. What will you choose to be now; continuing to be a follower, or becoming a leader? A creed is that which is believed; an accepted doctrine, a particular set of beliefs; any summary of principles or opinions professed or adhered to whereas religion is the belief in and worship of a supernatural controlling power, especially a personal god or gods. They are two different items on the list.

# DAY 13: STAGE 13

Are your prayers really being heard; let alone: answered? This God knows how to take the life right out of you. God Yahweh convicts us of our wrongdoings; what about him, who convicts him, of his wrongs, his mistakes, his lies, I do not fear this entity, and neither should you. He does not want us in heaven to begin with, so the hell with him. He expects us to live a gruesome life and love him; again, a psychotic way of thinking. You should have never needed to pray to begin with; if your God Yahweh was true as he claims to be, and already knows all your hearts desires, needs, wishes, he would provide for you without you asking. Instead, you are treated like a dog, begging and pleading for help and concern from a God who should have done better. (KJV)-Matthew 7:7-8 tells us; "Ask, and it shall be given to you; seek and you shall find; knock, and the door shall be opened to you. For everyone who asks receives; he who seeks finds; and to him that knocks, the door shall be opened." I do not have to ask; I know you have been let down time after time, even after asking and praying to this God. It is just words, empty words and promises. Yahweh does not pay attention to you when you participate in repetitive prayer, and prayer used along with physical items; such as rosaries, candles, chains, prayer beads, and jewelry. It is considered a dead prayer, but over 3/4 of the world prays this way. If you are going to do something, do it right! Prayer is a con, why should you pray for something that should already be given to you? He says he will provide for you needs, but then you have to pray, beg, and plead to get it. The world says when a man cry's, he shows weakness; the world is wrong; when a man cry's, he shows his true strength.

# **Religion is Corrupt**

The study of religion encompasses a wide variety of academic disciplines, including theology, comparative religion and social scientific studies. Theories of religion offer various explanations for the origins and workings of religion, including the ontological foundations of religious being and belief. Ever since the world began, man has demonstrated a natural inclination towards faith and worship of anything he considered superior/difficult to understand. His religion consisted of trying to appease and get favors from the supreme being he feared. This resulted in performing rituals and keeping traditions or laws to earn goodness and/ or everlasting life.

1. *Religion seeks power and position:*
You cardinals, priests, pastors, deacons, and clergymen standing behind the podium, who do you think you are? You believe you are powerful, don't you; well, let me be the first to tell you, you are not. Everyday a kingdom falls, and your domain is next, because your internal corruption and greed will and already has manifested itself. You are no different than a politician, ceo, or elected official. As soon as a little power goes to a person's head, it consumes them without ever realizing it. This is your small punishment, as the large one will soon follow. Religion is a man-made institution, just as is government and business; designed as a profit-making organization. Like any corporation, to survive and grow; it must find a way to build power and wealth to compete for market share, to the point of even harming society and leading them astray. I challenge anyone in a cult to start reading the truth, break yourself free from this.

2. *Religion anchors believers to tradition:*
The new and old age is a time of excessive superstition, racism, violence, misogyny, inequality, and ignorance. The subject of slavery has always had God Yahweh's blessing. People desperately sacrificed other people, animals,

and worshipped statues for favor with a God. A believer looking to excuse their evil behavior, sense of superiority, and planetary destruction can find validation in the bible, by the claimed writings of God. There are religious professionals who embody formal aspects of the religion and who act in positions of leadership and governance, and there are certain rituals reserved for them to carry out. The beliefs generate practical implications for how life should be lived. You have always wondered why things are the way they are.

3. *Religion versus Science:*

Are the Gods real, or just a myth? "Trust and obey for there's no other way to be happy, except through Jesus Christ." "The lord works in mysterious ways", preachers tell their flock, but these same men/women have been shaken to the core by the horrors of brain cancers, suicides, and divorce in their own lives, never recovering; going as far as seeking science to correct the matter. Science has evolved to tremendous levels in our age; only because the Gods allowed it to. Do you really think you can come up with these things on your own? I think not. The Gods interfere in our lives as they see fit. Without them, you could never develop and come up with the exciting terms of medicine we have today. But yet, you believe it is all you.

4. *Religion diverts generous impulses and intentions:*

How many times have you helped someone, only because it makes you look good, instead of out of the goodness of your heart? There is another tsunami in India, let me give so I can feel good about myself, only to never think or worry about these people ever again. This is what we do, the media shows a devastating incident somewhere in America or the world, and two weeks later, you have forgotten all about it. They can be dead or alive; you do not care, as long as you are living your life: who cares, right?

5.  *Religion teaches helplessness:*

Are you looking for a handout, or steadily working hard to provide your way through this world? Either way, it is out of your control. Droughts, poverty, floods, cancer, divorce, and financial downfall are all attributed to the will of God, and none of your design of structures, drainage systems, house pads, and strategic planning can prevent them. When it will happen, is when it will happen and there is not a single thing that you can do to avoid it. It has been tried through and through; man developing undeniable physical structures, only for the next hurricane or tornado to destroy it like it was made out of straw.

6.  *Religion promotes tribalism and separation:*

You think your religion is bigger and better than your neighbors: you hate him or her because of it. What foolish thinking. How do you think the Gods feel about that? Tribalism is the state of being organized in a tribe or tribes; simply put 'organized religion'. Religion breaks down relationships, instead of mending them, separating people from one another, which in turn, separates everything else from moving forward. Our world is barely holding on as it is, and everyone has an opinion about something, even you. Being in a secluded religion, blocks you from learning, and may even hinder you from making a new friend.

## **Why do you want to live?**

Everybody plays the tough guy until things get tough. I ask this question sincerely, 'why do you want to live'? Stop believing what everyone tells you and believe what you feel. Do not let God lie to you and tell you that he never meant to hurt you, because he did. Did you ever ask yourself the question of why you want to live? Seriously, truthfully, and honestly: why do you want to live, why do you want to be here? For money, children, fame, stature, happiness, to be a doctor, sadness? When you have these things, life is more tolerable; but not necessarily the case. When you do not have these things; life is hard and strenuous; but not necessarily the case. Anyone and everyone that sincerely tries to find god Yahweh ends up getting hurt.

Why are scientists hard at work finding ways to prolong life. It is no secret that no one wants to live forever, you already know why? I really did not have to construct these two books: you already know that the God's (Yahweh and Satan) are evil entities. Who wants to work forever, younger people keep getting annoying, be married to the same person forever, sickness and disease would never end, more people would show up on earth, your body keeps getting older, and you would have to learn new technology every couple years to name a few reasons. I curse the day I was born; and the happiest day of your life will be when you die. What is the point in surviving an accident when the direct result of it is hospital bills; physical and mental therapy; paying for damages; surgery; etc., all of which you probably cannot afford.

I say this because you are the author of your own history. A prayer is not to be answered: it is part of God Yahweh and God Satan's glory plan. When you pray to God, it is for his glory, you begging him for something you want or need. It will never be answered because, once again, it is not according to his will. This life is God's will, not yours; the destruction, chaos, murders, hurt, pain is all part of his will and plan.

Most people would say that I am wasting energy by writing this, I disagree; because you are wasting and applying useless energy by working, watching movies, sitting on the couch watching t.v., playing video games, going to a university, if you are a rapper/singer. The god Yahweh places so much pressure on you to be in a place called heaven, that never was meant for you. We have so many more opportunities to sin in this age than any other. "Sports as an idol, porn, phones, computers, vehicles, airplanes, romantic novels, musicians, the talking box-television, etc. Let me ask you a question, why do you love God? Have you ever asked yourself this question? I mean, really think about why you love God or hate God: what are your reasons? If heaven is anything like this earth, which it is, do not be fooled, I do not want it, would you? God Yahweh is the true liar blaming God Satan. Start now, think for yourself, do for yourself, when you bear one cross, you are asked to bear ten more: when you have given twelve inches, you are asked to give twelve more: when you get bored, you are told to find something to do: hell was designed for demons, not you, but you will be there with them. You will get a sip of water if you obey; tossed aside if you do not. You are tired of hearing it will be okay, but it never is. You will be burning in hell when you are not supposed to be!

Here is the difference: you believe that God is good, I know for a fact that he is not. He did not even have the decency to meet you, the appreciation to talk to you; one on one, or the civility to listen to your prayers; let alone answer them. You beg and cry for God to send his love down to planet earth and it never comes. You ask for the tears to be taken away and they never go away. Nothing changes, nothing improves, all you have is your reality! You keep saying that this person or that person is holding you back, no my friend: the person that keeps holding you back is God! Why should you have to settle for less, but yet, this is what you do day in and day out.

Devil number one occupies heaven; and devil number two lives in hell! How old were you when you first started hating yourself? That should never happen, but for some reason, it happens more often than not. For a God that claims to love you, life is rough, touch, right! Your arrogance comes from God Yahweh, yet he tells you to be humble. Your hate comes from God Yahweh, yet he tells you to love. Your un-forgiveness comes from God Yahweh, yet he tells you to forgive. Does this make sense to you?

Do you feel like you are stuck on a planet filled with morons? Of course you do! This is your loving God Yahweh at his finest. You have to share a life with the rest of the people that are here. Your God knew that you would not be able to withstand certain people and still put it into existence. From (KJV)-Genesis 3:17-20 says; "To Adam he said, "Because you listened to your wife and ate from the tree about which I commanded you, you must not eat of it: Cursed is the ground because of you; through painful toil you will eat of it. It will produce thorns and thistles for you, and you will eat the plants of the field. By the sweat of your brow you will eat your food until you return to the ground, since from it you were taken; for dust you are and to dust you will return." Why do you place so much emphasis on this life? You will not live forever.

I am not distorting anything. This is a God who created the earth for you and gave you nothing. Only your body. You have had to invent anything and everything of what you needed, only to survive. In my first book, I discussed about how things are reverse or backwards in this world of ours. Good is bad and bad is good. I need to add to this: here is an arrogant God, God Yahweh, who expects you to suffer, have heavy hearts, burdened thoughts, take the pain of this earth with a smile. Hope is an idea, a fantasy, a chasing of the wind.

God Yahweh knows he is wrong and still pursues his own righteousness. How many times have you tried to do right and become hurt behind it? And your brothers and sisters do wrong and succeed and live joyful lives. (QUR)-Book of Elevations 7:8-9 says; "The scales on that day will be just. Those whose weights are heavy-it is they who are the winners. But as for those whose weights are light-it is they who have lost their souls."

Why can't we just all get along?

# DAY 14: STAGE 14

Can you be comfortable worshiping an egotistical God?

You do so much wrong towards one another: your hand or dildo seems like the better relationship, respectively. To show you how selfish your loving God Yahweh is, he had his son say these things, coming from the (KJV)-Luke 14:25-26 and out of the mouth of Jesus Christ saying; "Large crowds were traveling with Jesus, and turning to them he said: "If anyone comes to me and does not hate his father, mother, wife, children, brothers, and sisters, yes, even his own life, he cannot be my disciple." This is your loving God people; telling you that you should hate your wife and family: how does this make sense to you?

The issue goes further down the rabbit hole than just having different sets of plumbing. For two species that are presumed to be made for one another, what has been the complication; entirely different, yet compatible? I guess it does work for a period of time, but not forever. If we cannot become rich in our lifetime; prosperous enough so that our grandchildren and great-grandchildren would never have to worry about money again, what would be next on the list. I believe the answer is love. We want to meet the love of our life, have companionship, communication, affection, closeness, devotion, and a lifetime connection. You are never the first to do something: what you do on a daily basis has been done for thousands of years, and will be for a thousand more. The world has always had 'man loving woman'; 'woman loving man'; 'man loving man'; 'woman loving woman'; did I cover it all. Unfortunately, love does not last, and we still cannot find what we want and need.

# What is the definition of love

First, let me say what love is not! # 1 - (Love is not when you want or need to be with your significant other every second of the day): love is when the time you spend with them is perfect, and the time you spend apart is equally as good. # 2 - (Love is not when you depend on them and your whole life revolves around them): love is when they are a perfect addition to your life, it doesn't make everything else seem perfect, it makes everything else bearable and manageable, they help you grow as a person, and make you a better person and feel better about yourself and life in general. # 3 - (Love is not when you hate saying goodbye): love is when you see "goodbye" as the possibility of saying "hello" all over again. # 4 - (Love does not cover their flaws): love shows their flaws for all they are, but you still love their imperfections, because it makes them who they are, and you love and accept them for everything they are. # 5 - (Love grows and encourages growth): love is not perfect but is always close to perfection.

*Insult to Injury:* You will and can never experience those five qualities mentioned above with your God Yahweh: so how are you ever expected to have this type of involvement with your significant other? We place certain qualities which highlight God's transcendence to show how vastly different a being he is from us, his creatures: but sometimes that distances us from each other even further. The quality list includes: God's independence (self-existence and self-sufficiency); God's immutability (entire freedom from change, leading to entire consistency in action); God's infinity (freedom from all limits of time and space: that is, his eternity and omnipresence); and God's simplicity (the fact that there are in him no elements that can conflict, so that, unlike us, he cannot be torn in different directions by divergent thoughts and desires). Theologians of every age have called these qualities 'incommunicable' because they are what makes God; well, God, an entity that has been alone for millions, billions, even trillions of years. He needs no camaraderie; he shares no intimacy; just a being out there, alone. While man, needs all these elements but cannot seem to develop and maintain a decent bond with one other; because the example was not laid out correctly. The blame is not on us.

## Characteristics of Man versus Woman

A man was never taught how to love; this is what he knows:

*John doe*; In my soul, I was told the true definition of a man was to never cry; work till you died, got to provide, always be the rock for my family, protect them by any means necessary, give you the things that you need. Nobody ever took the time to try to teach me what love was, I never trusted anyone enough to let him or her completely in my heart and mind. Our relationship suffers, trying to give you what I never had. I thought to always be strong, never let you think i care at all, let no one get close to me, that I'd never tell things to anyone else, just keep it to myself, never showing my affections and expressing my feelings: and everything would be fine.

A woman seeks love and to show appreciation; this is what she knows:

*Jane doe;* In my soul, I have so many emotions, and I want to share with my beloved one. I just want to be love unconditionally forever. I need you to be not only my lover, but my best friend as well. I do not want, I desire; open communication, honesty, trustworthiness, that occurs regularly and tactfully. You should take responsibility for your actions and behavior. I miss you being kind, patient, sensitive, understanding, adventurous, and compassionate. We need a man who wants to see his woman succeed in their life every bit as much as they want their own achievements. I would appreciate you holding my hand and me; without expecting sex in return.

It is not the man who chooses the woman; it is the woman who chooses the man.

# No Clue at All

Your loving God Yahweh does not know the first thing about love, relationships and friendships: and the God Satan surely doesn't either: and both set a bad example; so whom can we really learn from? Women hate this verse the most from (KJV)-Ephesians 5:22; "Wives, submit to your own husbands, as to the Lord." And men hate this verse the most from (KJV)-1 Peter 5:5; "Likewise, you who are younger, be subject to the elders. Clothe yourselves, all of you, with humility toward one another, for "God opposes the proud but gives grace to the humble." How can you show love to someone when you do not love yourself or feel loved by your own creator? God's pretended example of love; is to make you cry, be deprived, depressed, feel panic and anxiety, why should a woman expect a man; or man expect a woman to show any kind of commitment, love, faithfulness when their creator does not show it. Well, the first thing you can do is discontinue the matters of the world. Stop looking for someone that can provide materialistic things, items, and components for you, this is a dead end but is what our world has conformed to. Can we just love someone for who they are and not for what they can or cannot do for us, the world has gotten away from this system of finding an alley? Your heart may mature a few levels going this route. You know the saying; there are many Mr. Wrong's and Mrs. Wrong's, but only one Mr./Mrs. Right, if such concept even exists.

(Bad boys are never good; Good boys are never fun
Good girls go to heaven; Bad girls go everywhere
You should run off with the right one
But you never do, it's always the wrong one
Sometimes, you are afraid of a good thing when it comes your way
As you are only used to being sad, hurt, and lonely
You do not know how to react to a good thing
So you stick with what you know.)

# **Similar Brains?**

The difference between genders extends beyond what the eye can see. I have always felt within myself: for a species to have such a complex brain, why do we act so foolish; maybe this was another lie. Maybe we are not as smart as we think we are. The difference can be looked upon in four parts of the brain: processing, chemistry, structure, and activity. It just seems like the things made for good, end up bad; and things made for bad, end up good.

1. *Processing:*

Men use more gray matter areas in the brain, as women use more white matter areas. Gray matter areas are localized where white matter areas form more of a networking grid of connections. Can you picture the difference? Men are thinking and processing one piece of information and actions in specific, separate splotches in the brain; as women have a continuous pattern of connected diverse reflection. As if we needed anymore inconveniences between us; it begins with us thinking differently, therefore, causing disagreements, playing who's right and who's wrong, and you never grow together as one, always fighting each other on the simplest of topics.

2. *Chemistry:*

Chemistry is stronger in the non-sexual part of a relationship: if you cannot get this part correct, your sexual appreciation falls by the wayside. Way before that, there is the issue of testosterone and estrogen, which are obvious differences known to be dominant in a specific gender, but both carry these hormones. When it is high in the gender that it should not be, it causes physical problems, and when it is low in the gender it should be, it causes emotional issues. Do you see the dilemma?

3. *Structural Differences:*

'Structural' refers to the actual parts in the brain and the way it is constructed; including size and mass. Women have a larger hippocampus; which allows them to input and absorb more sensitive and emotional information. Men's are smaller, and tend to make them feistier and harder when affairs of love are concerned. Our right and left hemispheric divisions of labor are also contrasting. Females tend to have verbal centers on both sides of the brain, while males tend to have verbal centers on the left side only, and have fewer overall. You wouldn't think so, but these are all matters of contention that play a part in our relationships.

4. *Activity:*

The female brain tends to have more blood flow through it than a male. Why is this important you ask? More blood travels to a part of the brain called the cingulate gyrus: which gives women more emotional feelings. It leads women to be able to focus on more than one subject at a time; while men focus harder on one subject. This also plays into the problem of #-1 in this stage; the disparity is that #-1 focuses on problem solving, and #-2 focuses on emotional issues.

Why would a God design men and women to be so different, yet expect unity? You know my assumption! Sorry men, but according to these remarks, women definitely have a more complex brain. Remember I said that everything is opposite in this world; women should be in charge more instead of men, but who is instead? These points may seem simplistic to you; but it was designed this way on purpose, everything is on purpose, to make life harder for everyone. We wonder why our species do not operate smoothly between the two. Both parties need to hold equal responsibility in the dispute and quit playing the blame game: you are both wrong and misguided in your agendas. You enter into a relationship based off usage and lust; not love. Then have the nerve to blame your partner for all wrongdoings when things go awry. I believe that we are more in love with the idea of being in love than actually in love.

# The grass is always greener on the other side

God purposely placed strife between man and woman. (QUR)-ch 3, Family of Imran, v 6; and (QUR)-3, Family of Imran, v 57. The word desire means 'an attempt to usurp and control: women have a tendency to dominate her husband and man has a tendency to act as a tyrant over his wife. We seem to believe in this phrase even when we know it is false. This applies to every scenario in life, but I put it in this stage for a reason. How many have broken up with a person for another, and six months down the road, you recognize it was a mistake, since realizing what type of people are really out there? Then, you have too much pride and ego to go back and you end up missing out on a magnificent person, and settle for someone else. Alternatively, maybe it was a job, a friend, or other opportunity passed by. The feeling that the grass is always greener on the other side is experienced by people who believe that others have it better than they do: trust me, their life is no better. Remember when you could not wait to finish high school or college: now you wish you were back in this circumstance. Our human tendency is to look for something greater, do not be afraid to enjoy what you already have.

In 1545, Richard Taverner quoted the saying, "The corn in another man's ground seems ever more fertile and plentiful than our own does." Please stop falling for this misleading bait. The story of your life has always been 'busy, busy, busy: the world will not allow you to be happy, free, peaceful, and comfortable. What is the resolution then? I cannot tell you what to do, everyone's situation is distinct. All I can tell you is that it will not improve with another person or situation. The concept that 'happiness comes with less; miserable comes with more', is a true statement. They say that you will find love when you least expect it, this is not true, love could be staring you right in front of your face, and you missed it. Do not be like your God, and let something that can change the whole outlook of your life, pass you by. You have to figure this out for yourself, but I am trying to help you. Another piece of scripture from (KJV)- Matthew 10:37 says; "He who loves his father or mother more than me is not worthy of me; and he who loves his son or daughter more than me is not worthy of me." The book of 2 Edras in Apocrypha: tells of curses that is bestowed upon you for sins and actions that your grand, great-grandfathers, great-great-grandfathers, etc. did in their lifetimes. You are being punished for crimes you did not commit.

Something preached to you since you were young, is that you will meet the man or woman of your dreams, get married, have children, live a happy life; but then it doesn't turn out the way you planned/expected. Maybe it is not the best scenario anymore, or even since the beginning. Maybe being alone is better, but the gods gave you the opposite sex to keep the experiment continuing by having babies and having an appetite for sexual desires. Why is it easier for a woman to forgive her man if he cheats; but for a man, it is harder? You cannot satisfy yourself, how are you supposed to satisfy another? A fool for love is a fool for pain.

Stop having babies and buying homes/cars, thinking it will keep your mate there and fix the relationship. This will not do nothing, all you are doing is bringing more trouble upon yourself. If you have not corrected the issues before, material items or a new child will not solve your problem. This idea has never and will never work.

A man's reversed reaction to love is his actions; for a woman it is her mouth.

# DAY 15: STAGE 15

People in charge of the world; not the best idea we ever had!

We have no direction with God, what would make you ever believe that we are any better with humans leading the charge? When it comes to our worldly governments, we essentially have the 'blind leading the blind' scenario. We have all come to the conclusion that any decent human being could do a better job in a political setting, than the current list of representatives that hold office. I want to begin with the good ole USA, because it is supposed to have the perfect formula = a <u>democracy;</u> which is a system of government by the whole population or all the eligible members of a state, typically through elected representatives. You should call it the DSA, 'Divided States of America' because since the American Civil War; which was fought between 1861-1865, and 85 years after the inception of the USA, that is what it has been. We all know why this war was fought: to end slavery. At that time, there were 34 states in existence, and 11 of these states wanted to keep slavery. The others wanted to abolish it. This war placed family against family; I can only imagine the stress and weight of emotions during this era? First, slavery is a horrible origin in life. It has always existed, and is constantly allowed by your loving God Yahweh. (KJV)-1 Peter 2:18 says; "Slaves, in reverent fear of God submit yourselves to your masters, not only to those who are good and considerate, but also to those who are harsh." Are you confused, which God are we talking about; the allegedly loving God; or the profitable hateful God? Your good

God Yahweh made this particular statement. If he considers you a slave, no wonder your government does also.

You ask why would a loving God who claims to love his creation, place you into slavery and bondage? This occurrence continuously takes place throughout each generation born on this planet. (KJV)-Colossians 3:22 says; "Slaves, obey your earthly masters in everything; and do it, not only when their eye is on you and to curry their favor, but with sincerity of heart and reverence for the Lord." I feel terrible for you, if you believe in a loving God. Both Gods seem to be a heinous presence; no human being wants to be a slave to another, but yet here we are. Simply put, the two Gods rule over you, and we rule over each other, it is a vicious cycle that cannot be broken.

Since a young boy, I always wondered why we had 50 different states in our country; not the united states of America; all doing things out of unison. All having rules and laws separate of one another: different driving licenses, business laws, marriage laws, you do not know what you are doing. This is not a unified formula; this is a rift. And you wonder why governments fight across the board. This is why it has always been a 'Divided States of America' since the civil war. No one is trying to accomplish objectives in the same manner. We say different is good, yes, in individuality; but when it comes for the collective group of humankind, we need to be on the same page, and we are not. Why would the system be set up this way?

The USA was set up this way because it was never a country to begin with; it has always been a federation and a business ever since the end of the civil war. Each state is a business, run as a separate enterprise from one another; and your states governor is the headman. The presidential position is a scapegoat for the country. The president is in charge of nothing. In fact, the states were formed first in their individual formats; and then the country was formed to convince you and the world of unity.

Here is a country that does not pay its own debt, but requires you to. There are four essential characteristics of a state which include

1. Population
2. Territory
3. Sovereignty
4. Government

I know we are too involved in our daily lives to pay attention to the way things are really set up, or designed in the country of usa, but for your sake, I hope you start. The important point I want to make is in the subject of <u>sovereignty:</u> its definition is the authority of a state to govern itself, a self-governing state. And the definition of a <u>federation</u> is: a group of states with a central government but independence in internal affairs. If a state governs and manages itself, which it does, why do they need Washington. D.C.? Washington D.C. does not have any concern in the world for the 50 states.

The USA is only 242 years old as I write this in 2019. What you have studied in your history class are a book of lies. The majority of people believe that citizens left to escape the British tyranny. That is not the case. Whoever left and came to the new land from Britain; came to start their own rule of government and control in the new land. We know there were already people here, probably Mexicans, Cubans, Indians, but it was discovered by a guy named Christopher Columbus; how can something be discovered when someone already lived there, they found it, not you? Even a child has common sense on this subject. There are 30 other countries in the world that uses a system similar to the USA; but they call their areas provinces and territories. Only the USA uses the term 'state'; why is this? It is because a state tends to have a greater independence and rule of government within itself while a province is a region being ruled within a country.

But the (KJV) book of Ecclesiastes 1:9 says; "What has been will be again, what has been done will be done again; there is nothing new under the sun." Although we may see these issues in our age as new, it could not be farther from the truth. These issues that we think only apply to our

circumstances have been around since the beginning of time. Just in a different format. Homosexuals walk around like what they are; is new. You believe you were the first to be a corrupt politician, ha, the first was a long time ago before you were even a thought in your mother's womb! This has been going on for thousands of years, and you think you are special? Which begs the question, why doesn't God help more? Or even let these horrendous things take form in the first place? Everything God does requires a 'why'? All that you do, and all that you think you are; you will eventually fall off.

(KJV)-Exodus 18:21 says; "Furthermore, you shall select out of all the people able men who fear God, men of truth, those who hate dishonest gain; and you shall place these over them as leaders of thousands, of hundreds, of fifties, and of tens." You are only led to believe that you are voting for the one that you want to be in office. Every politician is already picked, groomed, and molded to not listen to you and obey what benefits the powers that be. You are always fighting a losing battle; how will you change it?

> Everything is a prison

## America: Satan's playground, the modern day Israel

The good God Yahweh chose the nation of Israel as his chosen people in the days before Jesus Christ arrived on the earth; and they are still his elected family. Israel was and is the flagship nation for the good God trying to represent good in the world, and how he behaves. Nevertheless, in the modern age; America is the chosen nation of the evil God, Satan;

being his flagship nation for the evil God representing an evil nature in the world. They are both copycats of one another; with us suffering the repercussions of their motives, and caught in the middle. Never has one country, the usa, given the world such evil and despicable ideas, processes, and design. From hollywood, porn, business, cars, internet, stock market, banks, drugs, cigarettes, prescription pills, music, incarceration, obesity, to healthcare; all these ideas were designed to destroy your spirit and soul. And the rest of the world follows what America does. What is the new trend in America is asked across the globe. That is not a good thing my friends. When you hear a politician saying "God Bless America", they are referring to the evil God Satan; just thought you should know. The good God Yahweh does not condone evil or violence, but allows it to happen, does this make him any better? The usa government allows drugs from Mexico to enter as part of their payment and then has the nerve to put you in jail for selling it and using it. The only reason marijuana is legal now; is because they found a way to legalize and tax it.

Your social security number is a plot to control you, have you figured this out yet? Government needed a simple way of tracking your movements. America is the format for the world that is to come, if it works here, it would work anywhere. Here are some facts you didn't know: the first three numbers are called the area number, the state you were born in; the middle two number is called the group number, representing where you are in the filing cabinet; and the last four numbers, are serial numbers issued consecutively within a group. A serial number: is defined as a number showing the position of an item in a series, printed on paper currency manufactured for purposes of identification. Only God Yahweh knows how many people are on this earth, in America, or in Australia. Why would the USA need to know how many people are here? It is so that the government could track you, enslave you with work, take your money, and use it for their benefit, leaving you struggling. Criminals have serial numbers, ssn is just a nicer way of saying it, but you are enslaved.

Simply put, man and woman's intentions in the world are always evil, always! Learn this quickly, if you do not know already. No one is out to help you, no one, and the least of all, the Gods. People in political positions across our globe learned this behavior from the Gods. The economy circulates by keeping you in debt (which you will never get out of); can you walk out your front door and appreciate a breath of air instead of worrying about your next paycheck; This country is a mess, and you are a mess; you do not realize it yet. Always remember, if it is too good to be true, it usually isn't.

## Yahweh's Israel; the chosen country

Yahweh is regarded as the good God in most parts of the environment; he has been known to have some appalling characteristics throughout history. He has always treated his chosen people of Israel like filth. This God has put them through slavery, disease, natural disasters, famine, etc. Everyone demands to know why Yahweh chose Israel as his chosen people and country with so many options to choose from. According to scripture, the reason why he appointed them; is because when he presented himself to the world, ideas, plans, and commandments, they were the first and only set of people who responded the way he needed and wanted. Everyone else rejected him. As the man 'Abraham' is to be considered the father of all nations. There, is the discernment; so you can quit searching for this answer. But even Israel obeyed, but then they disobeyed, and then came the punishments. Now this God uses punishment in a clever way. He says that he punishes you so that you can learn from your mistakes. There are many ways to learn from a mistake, why does hurt and adversity have to be an option? This is because he does not love you, and takes enjoyment in this particular course of action. Millions, billions, even trillions of people have rejected this God in regards to this bearing. The concern of persons asking themselves-why wasn't I good enough? The rest of the world felt rejected and with good reasoning; and don't you to some extent? Israel is the Divine plan of God Yahweh to the world in constant motion. Israel is to represent a balanced study of four elements: the selection, continuous testing, rejection, and replacement of the Jewish people. You are always being tested, how often do you fail or pass? As God Yahweh does to Israel, so does he to the rest of the world.

(QUR)-2 Heifer, v 145 says; "Even if you were to bring to those who were given the book every proof, they would not follow your direction, nor are you to follow their direction, nor do theyfollow the direction of one another. And ifyou were to follow their desires, after the knowledge that has come to you, youwould be in that case one of the wrongdoers.

1. *God is Impartial;*
2. *The Nation of Israel was preparatory;*
3. *Nation of Israel's favor was conditional;*

# DAY 16: STAGE 16

Dear God Yahweh,

I did not exist for centuries and centuries, and then one day I was born; fussing and crying, not knowing who I was, where I was, why the world was the way it is, and why I was living in this age and not at any other time in history. Since arriving from my mother's womb, I viewed the world and immediately knew that we were not created by a kind, loving, and just God, as most religions would tell you. Soon I became old enough to realize my senses; sight, hearing, smell, taste, touch, later beginning to talk, walk and run. Then I started elementary school, high school, and finally graduating from a major university. What do I do next; work for the next 50 years of my life and then die; I guess that this is our lifeblood and purpose. Life seems so boring; going through days, weeks, months, and years with the same repetitive conditions. I once asked myself, there has to be more to life than this; and I concluded, no, there isn't. I know you feel that this life was a waste, throwing in the towel with us, as I have given up on you as well; so why create it. God, the majority of the time, it seems as if you are making this stuff up as you go, just like us. I have come to the conclusion that you enjoy watching us suffer, grieve, struggle, weep, be confused, experience pain, and have strife with our fellow human beings. And you call yourself loving, but what kind of loving God is that?

I have to ask, why are you so cruel and angry towards your creation; humankind? When I go to church, everyone says that the devil, Satan is the evil one, but I think that it is you God, who is the evil one! Satan did not create this world, you did. He did not give us the laws we cannot follow, manage and maintain. In addition, by studying the bible, it says that the devil cannot do anything to my family or I without your approval. Therefore, if he wants to tempt me, confuse me, harm me, or kill me, he cannot do it without your blessing or approval. That verse says a mouthful; why do you want to hurt me, make me cry, cause me stress and agony? Why God, do you do these things to me, to us; what does this say about your intentions towards us?

Could you please stop the lying, and tell us the truth? The facts about why you truly created this abhorrent, loathsome world. I believe that you, God, were the first slave master, the first murderer, the first to feel pride, envy, gluttony, lust, hate, anger, sloth, and greed. Why do you pin these afflictions on another, when it is you; who is the representative of these conditions? I hate this world, as I know many others do as well throughout its course of history; it is so hard, hurtful, lonely, and filled with sadness, why would you do something so terrible to someone you claim to love. Did you lie to me God; when you told me that you loved me? Moreover, because you already started this, 'the creation', you could not turn back the hands of time, and not look back; continuing on with the lie. Is this life just a sick joke to you? There are days that I do not want to be here anymore, going through this each and every day.

You have all the power in the world to stop hunger, adversity, affection, and hardship; but you do nothing. Why do you not show yourself to us, and not through other people, but yourself? What are you afraid of? Are you afraid that we will not like you? Are you afraid that we will not approve of you? Some people in the world want to know you, but you conceal yourself. You reject the people who do well, and allow the evil to succeed. God, you have no shame or conviction in your heart. Your church is supposed to be a safe haven, but even there, the people who claim to love you but hurt others; friends, spouses, family, as they constantly damage, laugh, humiliate rape, molest, lie, steal, rob, and take advantage of other people. Who am I to trust, when I cannot even trust you? I seek and do not find, knock and nothing opens, I ask and never receive. Your priests, pastors, humans are just like you; wolves hiding in sheep's clothing.

God Hates You

What did you expect when you fabricated this world? By giving everything free will, did you really believe that everyone would love it, and obey your commandants? You knew better, and the opposite has happened, you expected a world filled with love and care; but you got a world filled with hate and anger. You have no one to blame but yourself. We did not ask for this world, but here it is, and here we are having to deal with it; no thanks to you. We are fighting each other, hating each other, and killing each other; all for an item called a dollar bill. Are you proud of yourself now, with what you have done? I have no respect for you; when you sit on your throne in heaven, and do nothing to help us. People need your help, but you have turned your back on us. Even going as far as giving this world over to Satan, as (KJV)-2 Corinthians 4:4 says; "Satan, who is the god of this world, has blinded the minds of those who don't believe. They are unable to see the glorious light of the Good News. They do not understand this message about the glory of Christ, who is the exact likeness of God."

I know in my heart God Yahweh, that you are the one that is made of true, indescribable evil. You knew that Satan would hate us and envy us, and wants only to kill, steal, and destroy anyone in his path; as you handed humanity over to him. You are not a father God Yahweh; you are an executioner, full of corruption, animosity, anger, and a bruised ego. What you did to us; is like putting a baby in a lion's mouth. You lied to us from the beginning, and never wanted us to live happy, peaceful, and joyful lives. Thanks for leading by example, when I see someone in distress, why should I help, when you do not. Why should I feed and clothe, when you do not, and when I can barely do it for myself.

I cannot say that I have ever felt love for you, and now, I feel as if I am slipping away, distancing myself further and further from you; because of the things you have said, and done. Maybe the young children love you, for now, but as they get older; they will see and understand what you have truly done to humanity, and they will not love you anymore. God, you are a domineering tyrant, who only does what you want, for your will, and not ours. You do not care if we are merry or sad, it does not mean a thing to you. You do not provide anything to cheer us up; we do it on our own. What do you want from us, because you say one thing, and do another? You put us in an environment that we were not quite ready for, and said go forward; just as a parent kicks an 18-year-old child out of the house. Just because he is legally 18 does not mean he is ready to tackle the world. He has no choice but to leave; and that is what you have given us in this creation, no choice in the matter. I know who you truly are now; and it makes me heartbroken to know that I was conceived by you. I, others, cannot change what we truly know and feel in our hearts. You may live in a fantasy world, but this is real life for us. You have no idea what we go through here.

Let your heart tell you what is true or not, never your mind. Your mind will deceive you because your mind reacts to what you see while your heart responds to what you truly feel. Surprisingly, many, many, many of you still do not understand this simple concept. I am worthless just as you are: only used as a pawn in the game of chess between God Yahweh and God Satan, an instrument. It was all good at first in the garden of eden because the two slaves did as god told them to do. As soon as adam and eve proceeded as they saw fit, all hell broke loose with God Yahweh. When god created man, he could never love you, as a so-called perfect being could never accept an imperfect person.

You as a people think that you are better than the next when you are worse. You portray one person in the world and a separate one behind closed doors. The hardest part of letting go is knowing that you were never in control of yourself in the first place. You believe you are but you are not. It is time to take your life back, you are not living, you are just surviving: time to take back your life from yourself, government, god, society, your spouse, parents. I am better than you because I acknowledge god for who and what he truly is; evil in all its forms and fashions. I do not try to outdo the person standing next to me, but you do; I do not care if your house is bigger than mine, but you do; do not care if car is fancier than mine, but you do; do not care about your money, but you do; clothes, menial tasks, education, : you humans are nothing better than a monkey in a cage.

Why should I fear you, you are not my friend. It seems that you are more of an enemy than my friend God Yahweh. So I stop fighting it and just accept it that the creator God who claims to love me is a liar, has the whole world in a strangle hold and will not let up until everyone obeys him. Why would I want to obey someone such as you? A tyrant, domineering, smug god? I cannot.

I wrote this letter to God at the age of 12; already knowing what was ahead for me.

Jeremy Lavergne,
Born: December/29/1979

# DAY 17: STAGE 17

How can you ever escape a lie.

Part of this subject is correct; we do have some sort of free will in our lives. However, it is not 100% true. Let me prove to you that God is deceiving you once again through this misconception. Let's say you have children, if you tell your children that they can do whatever they want, but, you give consequences to their action, it is not free will anymore. It is control at this point. If you tell your sixteen-year-old daughter that she has to be back in the house by 10 pm; and if she does not, she will have punishments to face the next morning. Free will would be letting her stay out as late as she wants without repercussions. By her knowing that she will have a punishment, she comes back at 10 pm; although wanting to stay out later and missing out on other experiences she was looking forward too. Without your demand, she probably would have stayed out until 12 pm or later. By setting an effect on her, it no longer becomes free-will. Can you understand?

And this is exactly what your good, loving God Yahweh has been doing to you; allowing you to believe that you have free will. But free will does not exist. If you obey his commandments, you get to go to a place called heaven that is supposedly happy; but if you do not obey his commandments, you get to go to a place called hell that is supposedly the opposite of happy. This is not free-will my friends, this is control. God Yahweh has fooled you, because in perception, he is controlling you by making you believe he is not controlling you. Whether you can conceive it or not; your self-consciousness has already made the decision for you already, about where you will spend eternity.

The God Yahweh says he understands our suffering; this entity has no clue what we go through, and if he did; to do nothing for us is cruelty beyond explanation. I will not give the Gods the satisfaction of crying or being depressed by them disappointing us, hurting us, making us miserable, and killing us: I suggest you do the same. This short life that we live is a complete joke, the little bit of happiness and peace that the average person experiences compared to his or her hurts, stress, pain, and struggles are ridiculous. The entity that created mankind is a selfish, controlling, possessive being. You are only lead to believe that you have freedom. You must find what you want through yourself, you will never get it from him. I say this to you, as I open up: I used to hate people and didn't necessarily love God, but now I love people and still do not necessarily love God. I see that we had no choice in our existence, our thoughts, our lives, our future, and our past. I love you, all who read this, I love you for you, and I speak to you about this, hoping you can love everyone else in the world despite his or her actions, because it is not their fault that they are the way they are.

Do not let these Gods get the best of you; you are greater than this. Many people have suffered the consequences of free will, original, secondary, and tertiary sin. The only person that can set you free is yourself. Original sin comes from Adam, and is transferred to you: by you committing a sin and it does not affect another person. Secondary sin involves when you commit a sin and it affects another, or someone else's sin affecting you. Tertiary sin involves three people being affected, and Quaternary sin includes four people, and so on and so on, you get the idea. In a way, you have control over another by your goodness or evilness. The more or less you sin, impacts a lot or none; realize this. (KJV)-Galatians 5:13 tells us; "You, my brothers and sisters, were called to be free. But do not use your freedom to indulge the flesh; rather, serve one another humbly in love." God is telling you to be free, but yet takes it back with a command and a punishment.

1. *Your spirit is confined to your body, for now:*

According to scripture, after your death, your soul/spirit will be free, but will be in one of two places. Why isn't it free right now, why do we have to be judged in the first place? Everyone has another identity trapped inside of him or her wanting to be released. You want to do or experience something so badly; but do not have the financial means to do it: or you want a particular woman; but she does not want you, because you are not handsome enough for her. This loving God lied to us; claiming to be a perfect entity, as there sure are many imperfections going around in this life. Your imagination is a beautiful object, but how many can actually follow through with them: imagination and your reality are two different beasts. You will never get what you desire, it was not in the plan. The sooner you come to this realization, the better you will be off.

2. *Prisoners in prison:*

I have no answer to the problem, but I have to say that living behind bars is not a humane position to be in. It was not my job, or yours, to figure this out; it was the God's responsibility to provide better opportunities for us, but they have failed us. I know that these people have killed, stole, raped, bribed, lied, and molested; but they should not be treated like animals. However, wait, isn't this your same God who said you are no better than an animal. Therefore, we should expect nothing less than what we see with our own eyes.

3. *Your place or residence:*

Please realize that you are in some sort of confinement and control no matter which way you want to look at it: you may have the ability to go to work, a store, shopping, a restaurant, or even visit a friend; but you are coming back to an either an apartment, condo, house, trailer, or townhome. You still have to look at four walls every night; you may have more than one set of four walls, but you get the picture. What makes it any different from a four-wall jail cell? Your ability and so called freedom to go to the store or cafe. That is a feeble-minded way of thinking my friend, I should expect nothing different from you. After your day of being out and about in the world; you are back to your 'limit of bonds'.

4.  *The matrix:*

Your sight, hearing, touch, taste, and smell give you the ability to realize the matrix. But blind and deaf people do not have such luxuries. And he still claims to be perfect: whatever. These people can never see a sunrise, a sunset, a bird flying, a lion eating a gazelle, water, air, but most importantly: themselves. That must be hard to take, to never see yourself. I cannot even imagine the feeling. I want to discuss the invisible word you must never know about: (control). Please stop watching reality shows, sports channels, strip clubs, worrying about the latest technology, and start paying attention to the bills and acts that are being passed in your capital cities. As mentioned earlier, I talked about the USA because all other countries are trying to model their system after America. I will not talk much on the subject, as I have given you people to research in stage forty. But they will and are trying to enslave you as I speak; it is time for you to wake up, you are called the masses, and a small percentage of the people in government: which includes federal, state, and local are doing a tremendous job of becoming closer to their goal, unless you start doing something.

Everyone wants to control someone else or something else. They want to be the boss, and having it any other way, such as having a situation spiraling out of control, is just not a safe and comfortable spot to be in. Be

honest with yourself, you are not living life; you are just surviving, barely. Wealth is in the mind, not the body. The small amount of politicians that think they run the governments and control things, are small in comparison to the masses. Protesting solves nothing, you protest in the street one day and years done the line, nothing has changed. I hate to say it, but violence is the only way to make a change. The government is violent with you, putting you in handcuffs, beating you, torturing you, leaving you jobless; masses, give them a taste of their own medicine and they will not enjoy it. Freedom and oppression live hand in hand.

Have you ever wondered why there are nine planets, but only one that has human life on it? I believe that the Gods had plans to colonize the other eight, but since we have also proven that we cannot get things right here on this planet; they figured why bother with the others. They are considered to be a waste if you ask me; we never can go on vacation to Jupiter, sunbathe on Venus, or visit your grandfather on Mars. They are just there, a useless, wasteful creation.

I challenge you to do the best you can and forget what someone else thinks, even God; that is all we can do.

# DAY 18: STAGE 18

Is your good, loving creator; God Yahweh a murderer?

Of course he is an assassin, just because he is the creator of all things: does not justify his right to kill as it does not for us. God Yahweh is an entity that loves to tell you what to do and how to obey, but cannot follow his own commandments and regulations. Is that the sign of a great leader? In most assessments, the answer is no. In the story of Noah, here is a God who does not give a care about what anybody else thinks but himself. This flood was in a time before Jesus Christ came to save the world. People were sinning and disobeying him so much, and was a very terrible time, that eventually led to God Yahweh deciding to send a flood to wipe out all of humanity. It rained for 40 days and 40 nights. He did not ask what anybody thought, but why should he, he is God; he answers to no one, he just did it. I assume some asked for forgiveness as they were drowning, but he did not save them. So the next time you beg for your life to be spared, or for some assistance in life; this is what he will be doing, (laughing out loud, lol). You wondered where acronyms came from, there you have it. The idea to wipe out humanity came from the good God, (men, women, children, and babies) and he did not care about them anymore, as he still does not care about you, as he can simply wipe you out in one blink of an eye as well; similar to throwing trash away and never worrying about it again. One pretends to be great and wonderful, but is really corrupt = the good God, Yahweh; and the other is straight evil and chaotic = the evil God, Satan. To be a great leader, you must obtain all of the following.

1. *Be a Great communicator:*

Does the good God Yahweh talk with you, acknowledge you, tell you things, or do you just sit in the church pew staring at the four walls until your time is up, running to get out of there? You think humans are not great communicators, shh…, we have nothing on God Yahweh, the most horrible communicator of all time. The bible is full of mixed and irregular messages. He has big plans for humanity, but the dismal part is that many humans, simply do not care anymore. I thought I was alone, feeling no emotion in regards to this God. I just wanted to finish out my life and be done with it. But I would never, ever give him the satisfaction of taking my own life, and you should not either; as that is what the good God Yahweh ultimately wants. One of the most important parts in being a good communicator is listening. Do you feel like this God Yahweh cares what you need, expect, feel, and what you crave; or are you are wasting time sending up prayers, burdens, and hardships to him: they go in one ear and out the other. No interest is given in correcting your problems on earth because he is the one who devises your obstacles to begin with.

2. *Good decision-making capabilities:*

Apart from having a futuristic vision, a leader should have the ability to make the right decision at the right time. Decisions taken by leaders have a profound impact on the masses. A leader should think long and hard before taking a decision but once the decision is taken, stand by it. The Gods do not play by these same decrees. This loving God Yahweh, that you sometimes praise, makes things up as he goes. Things were not going the way he wanted in the days of Noah, so he tossed a hissy-fit and murdered humanity. He did what he wanted and had no concern for your rights, longings, and aspirations. Only one man and his family was spared, the story of Noah, the ark, the flood can be found in (KJV)-Genesis 7:1-24. When the Gods designed this life: they had no intentions of making it easy, they wanted you and are pleased when storms, troubles, and difficulties hit your life and never go away. God Yahweh and God Satan never asked if you would enjoy this life, did they, they never asked for your opinion? And they never offered you the chance to say no; I do not want this. They just did it knowing it would be this way: this is not the sign of someone with good decision making skills.

3. *Accountability:*

When it comes to accountability, you need to follow the approach that says, "A good leader takes a little more than his share of the blame, and a little less than his share of the credit." What a charming description of words. This good, loving God 'Yahweh' takes none of the blame for sin, (which was fabricated by him), but wants an applaud and glory for conceiving the world you live in. Can you say anarchic or bi-polar personality? Unfortunately, we are screwed; we cannot make God do anything he does not want to do. You need a job badly, even praying for it, but it never comes. You want a nice companion, you go a whole lifetime and it never came. It is because he is not held accountable for anything, you are on your own. He wants to be given honor and glory for giving us breath, but how about a life where I can enjoy my time here, put food on the table, enjoy time with my kids, not worry about being murdered, resented, or stalked, etc. p.s.-He will never apologize for never sending you the perfect mate, career, etc.

4. *Honesty and Integrity:*

The supreme quality of leadership is unquestionably integrity. Without it, real success is never possible, no matter whether it is on a section gang, a football field, in the army, or in an office. Honesty and integrity are two important ingredients which make a good leader. How can you expect your followers to be honest when you lack these qualities yourself? This is why the world is screwed up the way it is. Take the blame for your mistakes Almighty God Yahweh and stop passing the fault on others. He never told you the truth from the beginning. Satan did not create sin: sin came from God Yahweh. Yahweh passes the blame of sin on Satan. You have to dig deep to find the answers to these amazing questions. If God Yahweh was the only being that was never created, as he claims to be, then everything: I will say again, then everything came from him. This means he, God Yahweh, invented every single thing in this universe; good, evil, and all that is in between. Where is his honesty, I'll tell you, he has none. He is not the only creator, there are multiple creators.

5.  *Commitment and Passion:*

Using a sports analogy, your team looks up to you and if you want them to give you their all, you will have to be passionate about it too. When your teammates see you getting your hands dirty, they will also give their best shot for you. It will also help you to gain the respect of your subordinates and infuse new energy in your team members, which helps them to perform better. If they feel that you are not fully committed or lack passion, then it would be an uphill task for the leader to motivate your followers to achieve the goal. The Gods demonstrate none of this. It is a continuous tug of war, and we, humanity, are trapped in the middle. If you do not clearly communicate your vision to your team and tell them the strategy to achieve the goal, it will be very difficult for you to get the results you want. Simply put, if you are unable to communicate your message effectively to your group, you can never be a good leader. Words have the power to motivate people, but actions have the ability to make them do the unthinkable. Who is winning the war between good and evil?

The good God has given up on this creation a long, long time ago. Is that a sign of commitment? He is patiently waiting till the end of this 7,000-year period to end, so that they can be done with it as well, and everyone will either be in heaven or hell, and then start over. He would have sent another extreme catastrophe to earth, if it were not for the promise to Noah. Not everyone throughout the modern world, however, accepts the story of Noah and the Flood, but I assure you, it happened. This good God sent a worldwide flood, killing everyone and everything that was not on the boat that Noah built. I don't know about you, but I cannot trust an individual like this. At the drop of a dime, he could strike you down with lighting, as he has done before. Look at how he is sending never before seen rain and snow storms, fires, tsunami's, heat waves, in our modern world right now. God Yahweh does not answer your prayers for yourself, why would he answer a pray sent to him by another for you. We have to be realistic on our thinking; and this is your god of love, care and concern; God Yahweh? (QUR)-Noah 71:11, God says, "I will let loose the sky upon you in torrents." And later on in (QUR)-Noah 71:13, he says, "What is the matter with you, that you do not appreciate God's Greatness?

This life is pointless, wasteful and useless; why do you give it so much effort?

# DAY 19: STAGE 19

Your body is the church; you do not need a building!

How many have you personally read, 2, 5, 10 of these books; and each of them have achieved absolutely nothing for you, right, they are just words? What about your friends and family? Still no help; that is what I hear. You are excited to start this big journey to change your life around, feel better about yourself, and granted, some do, but what is the eventually outcome down the road? You fail or fall off; and after losing 50 or 100 pounds, finally getting over a divorce, getting back on your feet after losing a job, or getting married for the first time, you are back to the same boring, daily, grind of life routine again; all of these activities has still left you filling unsatisfied!

(KJV)-Luke 6:26; "Woe to you when everyone speaks well of you, for that is how their ancestors treated the false prophets." Can I tell you why you will never be fulfilled or satisfied in your life? It is because your creator is not fulfilled and satisfied with himself and what he has created! Your loving good God Yahweh calls himself in (KJV)-Revelation 22:13; "I am the Alpha and the Omega, the first and the last, the beginning and the end". Any and everything goes through him, and by him, but this God is sadly, not delighted and gratified within himself; so how can you ever expect to be? We all know that a person who brags on themselves really has nothing to offer; rather, it is the man or woman who does not need to speak about what he or she has done who really has gratification and contentment in their inner self. This God Yahweh is saying and telling how great and wonderful he is in the bible; but it does not surface or come to pass in our physical world; if he was so excellent; he would let people talk about, and praise him on their own: and not by demand. The bible is 'whatever' with me; because, how was it written, God told man what to write and how to write it; it did not come from John, Matthew, Moses, or

Paul's thoughts and beliefs. Yahweh forced these men to write these words for him, that is what he does.

These types of books are a complete waste of time and energy if you are trying to find yourself. All these pastors and writers that write Religious books, self-help books, etc., are only interested in your money. (KJV)-1 Timothy 6:10 says; "For the love of money is a root of all kinds of evil. Some people, eager for money, have wandered from the faith and pierced themselves with grief." They do not give a damn if you were 3 seconds away from blowing your head off with a shotgun, or planning your 5 year olds birthday party. The bottom line is you have to find what is in your heart and soul, do not listen to anyone else, and find your personal love for yourself. I cannot tell you how to find it, and they cannot; even though they try. Because face it, you will probably never meet these people who write these book; so why invest time and energy in believing what they say, you cannot trust them. Pastors and priests are telling you how to love God; yet are cheating on their spouses and molesting young boys and girls. You are insane, if you continue to listen to these people, who do not follow the laws of God to begin with.

## Religious authors, Cardinals, Priests, Deacons

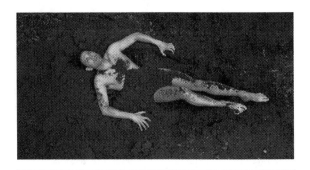

You are ash and to dust you shall return.

The gloves are off! What is the most important thing in this world? I would say love, family and friends, but not everyone thinks like I do. The most important things to them, you, is 'money' and 'space'. Even for these religious characters; the catholic church is the richest organization in the world, worth between an estimated $10-$15 billion dollars. The richest Christian, New Age, Baptist, Agnostic, Mormon, Scientology, Protestant pastors, etc., are all living in gigantic mansions, while you are struggling to make ends meet, still tithing ever week for your prayer to be heard by God. I do not claim to be a genius, but something seems fishy about this scenario. The bible speaks about putting investments back into the community and the helpless. Does your congregation perform these duties or is the money going to their next vacation? Is the money being put towards helping the homeless, the sick, and people in poverty, or is the church going towards selfish needs and causes, your pastors new bentley or pool, his mistresses? Be a leader; not a follower.

These people are the perfect definition of false prophets and scammers. Some have an idea, and some have no idea of what the good God is like; but tell you how to love, how to worship, how much to give (and criticize you if it is not enough for them), how to serve, how to pray, how to have faith, and how to sacrifice. I say to you; you are the only person that can judge yourself of how to accomplish these things, not Pastor Bob, or Sister Ann, only yourself. These persons do not care about you; after service, they are straying more than you, yet, judging you on your accords. This is all a game my friends, it is all simply a game being played. I want you to play the game, but win at it. They cannot tell you anything that you cannot find out on your own. God Yahweh has not called everyone to be in his service. And yet, we have a million and one priests, pastors, and clergymen; most of them, illegitimate. Using your lack of knowledge of our creators against you, making financial gain on your behalf.

## Self-help authors

Self-help books are the same; trying to teach you how to master finances, time, relationships, emotions; when these same authors lives are a catastrophe. Everyone is different, and no one is the same. When you finally have had enough of living the way you do, you will make a drastic change on your own, without no motivation from anyone else. No one can force you, no one can demand you; the only person you can control is yourself, and when you are ready to achieve it, you are ready. You, and only you, will know when the moment is right. Listen, I have been there, I have prayed to the good God, many times. When I received no answer, after no answer, I realized that I was on my own. The good God only replies to you when he wants to. The only person that will take care of me and have concern for me; is me.

## Phycologists, Relationship Experts and Life Coaches

Do you consider yourself to be a smart person? I do, and if you do as well, then why would you consider taking advice from a marriage counselor who is divorced three times, or listen to a life coach who needs one herself, a relationship expert who has never been in a rapport for longer than six months? These people's lives and affairs are in a state of disorder, and you want to listen to them. You know who you are, and no one else can tell you this. Believe it. Stop looking at what the world has to offer; because what the world has to offer, is 'garbage', in every sense of the word. The television tells you that you need this, it's not true. Your mom, dad, says you need to do that, it's not true. You wish to have this amount of money in the bank or need to have this person fit 'your type' to be in a great relationship, it's not true. Be brave, only you can tell yourself what you need to start feeling secure, content, and happy. Let the world and everything in it go. It will be hard, because we have become accustomed to a way of living now. The I want it now attitude; trust me, you don't really need it. Do you and stop worrying about everyone else. I will be authentic with you. I don't know if a person can ever be completely elated here, but it is worth the try. You can fool everyone else, but not me, you are not happy; and the reason I know, is because I was not happy. It is just the way it is, I'm sorry, it is the way this world, our world, was designed for us. I am telling you these things because I love you, I have never met you, but I love you. The best we can do is the best we can do, and be convinced that we have done our best.

I have become so sick and tired of reading these books about finding the meaning of life, what is your purpose, love yourself first, be the best person you can be, philosophy on life, laws of power, etc. You keep filling your mind up with garbage on top of trash. Tidying or cleaning up a landfill still makes it a landfill; it is still full of junk, just organized junk. These types of books do not discuss the real issue, they avoid it. I have examined each of these topics; but have told you about the root of the problem. I have excepted that the Gods hate me, and I have moved on. Realizing that their opinion does not matter, to me or anyone else. You can never please something that is never happy or elated. So the minute I stopped trying to please either God, I became a nicer, and better person. (KJV)-Ecclesiastes 5:10 says; "Whoever loves money never has enough; whoever loves wealth is never satisfied with their income. This too is meaningless." You are the church: your mind, body, heart, and soul is the church. You never needed some priest or pastor telling you who and what God is, you already know. All you ever had to do was look inside those four characteristics and you find him. But you would rather spend your time and energy on the foolishness of this world/life.

When Jesus Christ returns to earth for the second coming, he will be coming for his bride-'the church'-which is you. But who is taking care of the church. Churches across the globe are corrupt, pastors/priests/congregations do not know the word of God and are sleeping with men, women, and children, molesting, using tithes for unethical purposes, lying, tell you what you want to hear and not what you need to hear!

Let us make you thing certain, I do not need some piece of paper from a religion saying that I am a pastor, priest, brother or nun etc. and neither do you. The truth is: all you need is a relationship with God Yahweh and God Satan. Do you find that last statement confusing? You should not, and to clarify again, they work together in unison seeing whether or not you will sin. I have a relationship with both. I, you, cannot escape the fact that they are there, that they exist.

Do you finally understand that the church is not a building, it is inside of you!

# DAY 20: STAGE 20

The good God and evil God are distant to you on purpose, and on their terms.

In (KJV)-Matthew 18:2-6 Jesus says; "He called a little child to him, and placed the child among them. And he said: Truly I tell you, unless you change and become like little children, you will never enter the kingdom of heaven. Therefore, whoever takes the lowly position of this child is the greatest in the kingdom of heaven. And whoever welcomes one such child in my name welcomes me. If anyone causes one of these little ones—those who believe in me—to stumble, it would be better for them to have a large millstone hung around their neck and to be drowned in the depths of the sea." This contradictory God Yahweh does not love adults, but we all eventually become adults. The reason he does not care for adults is; we become too smart, wise, and knowledgeable for our own good. As grown-ups, we think we have it all figured out. Children barely know anything. This goes back to 'The Garden of Eden' when he wanted to keep Adam and Eve not knowing very much, with brains like a marshmallow: then Satan came along and said, "that's not fair to them, as Adam ate the apple and became intelligent." The good God Yahweh wanted you as pets; simple and plain. Satan saw much more potential in you.

Even though he created you, he expects you to seek him. (KJV)-Proverbs 8:17 says; "I love those who love me, and those who seek me find me." So there you have it ladies and gentleman, the facts; if you do not love God, he doesn't give a care in the world about what happens to you. I am a nobody, by worldly standards, a simple man; but in my opinion, if a creator molded me out of clay, shouldn't he be seeking me; I did not ask, you did not ask, nobody asked to be here, we did not ask for this world! However, it is just the opposite; as you should not expect anything different from a narcissistic creator. He wants glory and honor for this creation. What do you want God; do you want a pat on the back saying 'congratulations', you are so wonderful? Nevertheless, I simply cannot give him glory; not when he allows people to kill babies in the womb, rape and kill, people born with deformities, exiled from your country, you develop cancer, people are born blind, and the list goes on forever and ever.

I am tired of everyone blaming the evil God-Satan, when something bad happens in their life, it's always the evil God's fault; wake up citizens of the world. The good God is to blame as well. It is time the good, so-called loving God step up to the plate and takes responsibility for his actions. He is responsible for all the insanity in the universe; but passes blame on others who had nothing to do with it. I really hope you are receiving something out of reading this; because I am happy to present this information to you. The whole world is confused, not knowing the truth. Why were Adam and Eve so lucky? They were lucky, in the sense; to have at least spent some time with the loving God and the evil God. You know the story. We were not so fortunate to have that time; we are billions of people on the planet, and trust me, he has proven he cannot look after everybody, and doesn't want to.

Churchgoers, who go to church on a weekly basis, have empty souls. Do not let them fool you, having you believe that they are happy, they are pretenders. No my friends, these people are worse off than you, living a life to please a God who doesn't give a damn about them. They go to church because it is routine, tradition, and they are trying, really hard, to understand God, and their purpose, to their last breath. God says he has a purpose for you here, but chances are, you will go your whole lifespan never knowing what your true purpose was. What a life, right!

## Relationships

On earth, where we live, would you agree that some relationships are not worth keeping? You would not be best friends with a murderer if you knew that they killed someone, would you? Or stay with someone who keeps beating you. Or someone that keeps stealing from you? Your loving God Yahweh says that relationships are worth restoring. (KJV)-2 Corinthians 5:18 says, "God has called us to settle our relationship with each other." Do you agree with this? Many times, you are better off alone, than with someone that keeps hurting you; emotionally and physically. You have to break the ties, no matter how difficult it may be. But this good God tells you to restore it, staying in the affair; staying in the hurt, maintaining the black eye; to keep being used and broke. The bible says that when you ask God to forgive you, he forgets about your sin; the problem with that is, by the time he forgives you, you have done a hundred more sins, have you thought about that before. This does not work with God; we cannot escape this.

Yes, God is real, no matter how much you hate it. The hardest thing to do in this life is to accept that you did not create yourself. Deep in our souls; we want to control every aspect of our lives. And to a certain point, we do, but it is hard to welcome the fact that you were created from something else. And you never met this 'something else' yet. We want to believe that we always existed and that we control our destiny. Not knowing if you will live to be a 100 years old, or 50, is a scary thought. Do I have my retirement set up; are my children and grandchildren going to be okay after I am gone; the best years of my life are done, I'm on the back 9; what happens after I die? It is always the easiest to worship God when things are going wonderful and abundant in your life, when he has provided happiness, food, clothes, friends, family, health, and situations. But circumstances are not always pleasant. How do you worship God then? What do you do when God seems a million miles away?

The good God promises in (KJV)-Deuteronomy 31:8 says; "It is the lord who goes before you. He will be with you; he will not leave you or forsake you. Do not fear or be dismayed."; yet he also never promises that you will always feel his presence! Don't they belong one in the same; if someone tells you that they will always be with you, you will also feel their presence, even if they are 1,000 miles away? But apparently it doesn't work like that with the good God. He wants to tell you that he will be there for you, and still, when you call for him, feels like he is a million miles away. Because he is a million miles away! He is too good for this earth. It's too dirty and disgusting for him.

Many pastors across the globe don't even understand it, can't explain it, 'who, by the way, are supposed to be the disciples of the good God on this earth', describe it as: "You wake up one morning and all your spiritual feelings are gone. You pray, but nothing happens. You rebuke God Satan, but it doesn't change anything. You go through spiritual exercises . . . you have your friends pray for you . . . you confess every sin you can imagine, then go around asking forgiveness of everyone you know. You fast . . . still nothing. You begin to wonder how long this spiritual gloom might last. Days? Weeks? Months? Will it ever end? . . . it feels as if your prayers simply bounce off the ceiling. In utter desperation, you cry out, 'What's the matter with me?'" Can I tell you; that nothing is the matter with you. You just have a self-proclaimed good God who put you on this planet, and wants you to go to him, when it should be the opposite. But you can try these things.

1. *Remember what God has already done to you.*

This is a God who has given you a dreadful life to live in with no apologies; and wants to make it up to you, by the means of offering his son 'Jesus Christ' on a cross. Guess what Yahweh', it doesn't make up for what our life is like now; the never ending struggle, the constant worry, and the stresses of maintaining our needs. We, as a universe, are still dealing with hurt, loneliness, sadness, hunger, concern, bills, etc. Some people claim that even If God never did anything else for you, he would still deserve your continual praise for the rest of your life because of what Jesus did for you on the cross. If you, 'the good God', are the one true creator of the universe and answer to no one, I can't see the point in having to send Jesus to die for our sins; it is frivolous. He always gets somebody else to do his dirty work and clean up all his messes. It seems something better could have been done. Yes, we do easily forget the cruel details of the agonizing sacrifice that Jesus made on our behalf, but it was an unnecessary act. Here are the accounts of the event; even before the crucifixion, the Son of God, 'Jesus Christ', was stripped naked, beaten until almost unrecognizable, whipped, scorned and mocked, crowned with thorns, and spit on contemptuously. Abused and ridiculed by heartless men, he was treated worse than an animal. Then, nearly unconscious from blood loss, he was forced to drag a cumbersome cross up a hill, was nailed to it, and was left to die the slow, excruciating torture of death by crucifixion. While his lifeblood drained out, hecklers stood by and shouted insults, making fun of his pain and challenging his claim to be God. Yahweh, the good God, all powerful and magnificent; this description of death is very grim, hideous, and repugnant, was this the best you could come up with?

2. *Tell God exactly how you feel.*

Worse my friends; is that you can always expect the unexpected. You can try pouring out your heart to God, unloading every possible emotion you feel in the world. You have probably attempted this already, but to no avail. You end up answering yourself, and your own questions. He doesn't care how you feel. You can keep on sending prayers to this entity that never get answered or you can make it happen for yourself. He will never give you what you truly desire; you make it happen.

3. *Focus on who God is—his unchanging nature.*

Yes, his unchanging nature, an unchanging nature that hates and despises you. This is true, God Yahweh's nature never changes; and to the point: we are wasting time trying to speak with him. (KJV)-Numbers 23:19 says; "God is not man, that he should lie, or a son of man, that he should change his mind. Has he said, and will he not do it? Or has he spoken, and will he not fulfill it?" Yes, he does not lie, knowing that his will and your will, will never align, therefore doing what he wants first: you becoming frustrated and veering out to do things your way. His unchanging nature of giving no relief and help.

4.  *Trust God to keep his promises.*

First of all, the good God Yahweh has promised you nothing. He did not say I will provide you with the biggest house; the best clothes; money; fame; success: the only thing he did promise is death. And that is a promise he will keep, the rest, not so much. (KJV)-Romans 6:23 says; "for the wages of sin is death; but the gift of God is eternal life through Jesus Christ our Lord." Who wants to live forever? Not me; we were given something that we never wanted and never desired. You will live forever though: you will have eternal life being God Yahweh's slave in heaven, or God Satan's captive in hell.

We live in a hell on earth, and in eternity.

# DAY 21: STAGE 21

I wish that you would discover how Yahweh and Satan: both play with your life.

How can you feel comfortable building trust with this God Yahweh when he tears it down, throws you under the bus, does not treat you fairly and you suffer for no good reason? I just want to iterate that it does not matter who and what you think you have accomplished or not accomplished in this world to them: I have known people with million-dollar homes, money, and success; and are the loneliest, saddest people on the face of the earth; and I have known people with barely ten grand in their bank account, a modest home, but live blissful and content lives. No one cares what you have, or have obtained in this life; because it will be stripped from you, I promise you this. You will spend more time lying in a coffin than walking the earth, so I ask you; what is the point in obtaining material item after material item? I chuckle at people who have this mind set; that nice suit and dress you will wear at your funeral will be looking fabulous six feet in the dirt where no one can view it. You need to finally get your priorities right, while you still have time!

God Yahweh creates purposeful evil on this man; it was not the result of this man's free will. The story of Job invites us to consider what it means when God tells us he rules the world by wisdom, cruelty, and how these truths can bring peace in dark times, but this is, yet another lie. Set in a time before Jesus Christ, in a land named Uz, an obscure place located far to the east from Israel: the book of Job focuses on questions about God's justice, injustice, and why good people suffer. But you will soon realize by reading this story: the God Yahweh is being boastful, prideful, and egotistical, using Job's life and pain as a sacrifice to his own glory. This is the case of our creator claiming to be caring and loving; but in reality, is about God's rivalry, conflict, and enmity with the evil God Satan. Job was a wealthy man with a peaceful family, money, status, and extensive animals. He was considered to be well respected in the community; some going as far as charactering him as a "blameless" and "upright," man, always careful to avoid corruption, from (KJV)-Job 1:1. (KJV)-Job 1:2-3 it says; "He had seven sons and three daughters, and he owned seven thousand sheep, three thousand camels, five hundred yoke of oxen and five hundred donkeys, and had a large number of servants. He was the greatest man among all the people of the East". In other words, he had the perfect life; by our worldly standards. You can read more about this subject in the chapter Job in the (KJB).

If you did not know, Satan can travel back and forth, in and out of heaven, but God will never go to hell. So one day, Satan ("the Adversary") appears before God in heaven. God boasts to Satan about Job's goodness, but Satan argues that Job is only good because God has blessed him abundantly. Satan challenges God that, if given permission to chastise the man, Job will turn and curse God. God allows Satan to torment Job to test this bold claim, but he forbids Satan to take Job's life in the process. Satan takes everything leaving only Job and his wife alive. God Satan, 'the devil', killed Job's sons and daughters; set fire to his home; let his animals die; and left Job bankrupt. Job could not understand why his loving, kind, and so-called compassionate God would allow such a thing for him: his wife, finally telling Job to curse God and be done with it.

The good God Yahweh likes to pretend that these evil and destructive situations that develop in your life come from Satan; but any logical and reasonable person with a brain can see and visualize that they really come from God Yahweh. Yahweh could have said no to Satan, leave him alone, but he did not. You must read between the lines, and have a heart of understanding to see these positions. This God Yahweh just sat back and watched Job get battered, mauled, children dying, be mentally abused while not doing a single thing to stop it. Yahweh gave permission for Satan to harm and take everything in this man's life, except his death. If God Yahweh would have said take his life, it would have been done. The God's still treat you, your family, friends and colleagues in this exact manner; even after thousands and thousands of years. The game never changes, only new and different souls/minds to play with.

It is no wonder your loving God Yahweh lets a father molest his only daughter; men and women be prostitutes, raped and killed; you try the stock market and lose all your finances; children being sex slaves to adults; let a young child be born with a chronic disease and never live past the age of 5. I am here to tell you, my friends: that they come from your good, loving God Yahweh. He is the liar, the fraud, the fake, and backstabber. Satan can only tempt you; but Yahweh is the one who allows it to go through without preventing it.

God Yahweh allowed this man Job, you, your friend, cousin, aunt, or mother: to experience a burden that is so great to bare, that they consider suicide. Job was on the verge of suicide, and I believe that he did curse God. What a cruel and grim God: all for the sake of proving his point, to have his glory, and to be worshipped. I always thought to myself, if you are God, 'with great and amazing powers', why do you need meaningless praise from a human being? Aren't you above that? What we are dealing with my friends, is a God who has low self-esteem, lacks confidence, and needs; not wants, needs praise and worship from us lowly human beings. We talk about our neighbors needing attention and consideration: it is not even remotely close to the God Yahweh.

Sometimes I wonder why I try to stay fit. I can easily die in an unfortunate accident next week, and someone that is living a fraudulent life can live for another 40 years. I came across a story in 2014 about two women that I will never forget and would like to share. They were both 100 years old at the time and had been friends since the first grade; 94 years of friendship. Someone asked how they became to be that age together; if there was some secret schedule that they were keeping from the world. One of the 100-year-old ladies said 'I did not smoke, drink, cheat, or do drugs my entire life', and the other lady said 'I did all of that, and I am still here'. I thought this was so funny, but painstakingly true about our lives. It does not matter to the Gods. You can be on your way to success, and then, nothing, your life ends because it is out of your control. (QUR)-The Shattering 82:7-8 tells you that; "he who created you, and formed you, and proportioned. In whatever shape he willed, he assembled you."

The story of Susanna in the book of Apocrypha entails two men of the priesthood who found the woman Susanna very beautiful and sexy. They spied on her day in and day out as she bathed, did things around the house, and dressed. The two priests couldn't take it anymore, they had to have her, so they approached her for sex. She denied them, and then they twisted the story saying she came on to them. They figured that since it was 2 against 1, that the community would believe the priests. This is your God people.

Will the real wolf in sheep's clothing please stand up?

# DAY 22: STAGE 22

Inhabitants of the earth have always hated God right back.

I cannot provide all the answers for you, because I did not create whatever this world is. If I did, I could give you what you needed. The one who did create this does not give you what you need and want. Your Gods heart is not genuine: it is fraudulent and venal. They hide themselves from you, never to be seen in plain sight. I always believed that you could never trust someone that did not look you in the eye! Does God Yahweh or even God Satan look you in the eye? They have all the time in the world, but you do not.

Love is pain; and pain is love. If you vision yourself as the first person, ever, to hate God and curse him, you are wrong. It has never been a good relationship between humankind and God. A world filled with question after question; rarely being answered. We are two different, opposing beings. He acts like he understands and recognizes what we go through, day by day, hour by hour, minute by minute, and second by second on this planet; but he does not have the first clue on how hard it is to live on this earth. The Gods thought this was a wonderful idea; but they were wrong. We have no self-identity in ourselves anymore. I have seen people of all ages believing that a particular tattoo represents who they are. And what about parents living their dreams through their children. Or finding self-identification through movies, music, money, sports, vehicles, clothing, a job, jewelry, hairstyles, and status quo. That way of thinking is humorous. I cannot tell you how to find yourself, this is something each and every individual on this sphere needs to do for one self. Only you can do it, God will not help.

I use America as the example, because it is what most countries aspire to be like. We, as a culture in America, can say we have it pretty easy; compared to second and third world countries. But who said America or any other country is a first world country? Life is not fair, and the majority of people get the wrong end of the stick. In America, we live in a dog eat dog society where people are not human anymore. They only care and worry about themselves-selfishness, and most of the world follows our example. Whomever is reading this across our globe, can we try and present; being a humble, kind, temperate, faithful, loving, giving, and diligent. In (KJV)-Matthew 5:38-40 Jesus tells us; "You have that it was said, 'eye for eye, and tooth for tooth. But I tell you, do not resist an evil person. If anyone slaps you on the right cheek, turn to them the other cheek also. And if anyone wants to sue you and take your shirt, hand over your coat as well." This analogy does not sit well with our world view, if someone slaps you, you are going to respond by slapping them back or getting revenge in a new way.

## **This was all just an experiment**

An experiment is defined as: an investigation in which a hypothesis is scientifically tested = ("tree of knowledge of good and evil" and "tree of life"). In an experiment, an (independent variable = the cause = the good God, 'Yahweh') is manipulated, and the (dependent variable = the effect = the evil God, 'Satan') is measured, and any (extraneous variables = subjects being controlled = human beings).

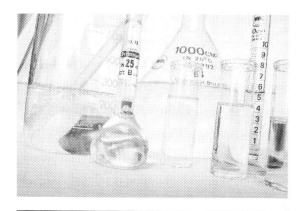

You are just an experiment
gone horribly wrong.

You are just an experiment, I was an experiment, all the people who have lived before and after you, were just an experiment; an experiment gone wrong. The angel examination is different from human beings, as people are a different observation from animals. We all have separate distinctive traits, and perform different objectives from one another. The sooner you realize the truth, the better you will be, that we were not created out of love as is the story told, but rather, as a cold-blooded undertaking. Angels were the first, then our world, dinosaurs, Adam and Eve, and finally animals.

The experiment went terribly wrong in the days of Noah; so the Gods sent a flood to wipe out all of humanity, saving only Noah, his three sons, and their families. He would have done it again, and again, starting over and over again, except by the grace of this guy Noah; asked him never to do this again. I have heard pastor's say, "God's purpose is to save us, not tinker with us." This flood was an example of tinkering; like pressing the re-start button on PlayStation. He intervenes when he wants, takes your life when he wants, and doesn't help when he wants.

The experiment is almost over. What have you done with your life? I believe no one is completely satisfied with what they have or have not accomplished during their time here. I cannot stress the importance in noticing the conflicting emotions that we deal with. The good God says he gives us peace, saying in (KJV)-1 Peter 5:7 says; "Cast all your anxiety on him because he cares for you." I have tried this, giving God the benefit of the doubt. But you know what happens, and I am sure you will agree. Once one situation is handled, I have another seven that I have to deal with, and that first one is not completely dealt with. This good God tells you what you want to hear, that's all. If you believe in an all almighty God, you should be past upset with him. All he does is uses you, for his pleasure. Let me paint the picture. If this God created Lucifer, who became Satan; God allows him to tempt you, destroy you, steal from you, and kill you emotionally. You are but a pawn to God.

## **<u>Not Yours</u>**

I am fascinated by the fact that you accredit this world as yours. Instead of making the world a better place for generations to come, you only think about yourself and the 'now factor'. You do not even own yourself, but walk around with pride as high as the sky. If this God Yahweh said to himself, no more, you would fall down and die right where you are, as your breath is removed. What is stopping him from doing this now? The 7,000-year-plan stops him from doing it now, it has to stay its course, the time is not up yet. When will you learn my friends, that it is not about you, it never was. It is hard, I know, to come to grips with your God not loving you, so how do you move forward. Try to be the nicest, kindest person that we can be, do not be like the Gods, full of hate: and unfortunately, we act just like the Gods.

You think that your piece of property is yours, you covet it;

You sleep with another man or woman's spouse; you commit adultery;

You lie to stay out of trouble and put another in harm's way, you bear false witness;

You value money, vehicles, and clothing above all else; you have many Gods;

You make items for self-enjoyment which never satisfies your thirst, graven images;

You live two blocks away from your parents and have not spoken in years; no respect for your origin;

You murder, spill blood, without an afterthought; killing

You do not respect rules and regulations; the Sabbath

You take what is not yours from another; stealing

You secretly desire to be another person, but cannot admit it; you covet their goods

From the Apocrypha; the book of the song of the three holy children: God Yahweh allows three innocent children who loved him deeply to be murdered and slaughtered on account of their faith.

# DAY 23: STAGE 23

People do not want to be caught in the middle of something for very long. It is difficult and awkward to maintain.

The older we get; you would think we would learn more, but it is the contrary. (KJV)- Ecclesiastes 1:18 says; "For with much wisdom comes much sorrow; the more knowledge, the more grief." From (KJV)-2 Timothy 1:7 tells us; "God has not given you a spirit of fear but of power and love and a sound mind." God Yahweh is mentally unstable, what do you think would happen to you? The world is hurting with this issue; among others, with no sign of relief in sight, so the good God Yahweh lies once again. This phenomenon of mental illness is one of the worst things that a person can deal with in their life; to put it mildly, it tears and stretches your brain apart, piece by piece, day by day. The stress and headache never stops, never goes away, and never ceases, it just keeps on hurting. Yes, medicine does help some, but it is not the permanent fix that we are desperately seeking. We are not perfect human beings and cannot create perfect things. Nevertheless, if you have ever been through the medical system before, you know that the medicine eventually wears out. You eventually need stronger and stronger doses as time wears on. Another scenario is that you lose your job and your insurance is cancelled; leaving you unavailable to afford prescriptions any longer. Neither one of these are good options for your body.

In addition, the medical industry does you no favors. I can speak from personal experience, as psychiatrists who worked for both departments once treated me: in both the public and private sectors. Names will be withheld, as both doctors have resigned, individually, in the state of Texas because the authorities in the public sector, told all doctors to give only fifteen minutes per patient. They needed higher turnover ratios; and were never concerned with actually listening to the patient's problems. They do not treat you like a person; they treat you like a number, as this is a multi-billion-dollar business.

1. *Schizophrenia:*

Schizophrenia is a severe mental illness characterized by a person experiencing a combination of delusions and hallucinations. Because these delusions and hallucinations feel as real as the world around them, a person with untreated schizophrenia can sometimes have trouble distinguishing actual reality from this altered reality that their brain is telling them they are experiencing. Many times, the world calls these people crazy, right? But the truth is, they are in a better reality than people that are considered normal. People suffering from this disease can see anything from angels and demons, to hearing voices, and an altered sense of self; serious changes in emotions, movements and behavior.

2. *Astral Projection:*

Is an un-willful, or willful out-of-body experience that assumes the existence of a soul or consciousness called an "astral body" that is separate from the physical body and capable of travelling outside it throughout the universe. This particular symptom is not as common, according to statistics, as others are, but extremely dangerous to the mind and its stability. 90% of the people, who I have encountered with this particular symptom, claim that they never tried it on purpose; they just did it, subconsciously. I advise anyone not to learn this; as it is very dangerous and can mess with your mind and brain intensely.

(KJV) the book of Ecclesiastes 12:6-8 says; "Remember him, before the silver cord is severed, and the golden bowl is broken; before the pitcher is shattered at the spring, and the wheel broken at the well, and the dust returns to the ground it came from, and the spirit returns to God who gave it. 'Meaningless! Meaningless! says the teacher. Everything is meaningless!" The teacher in the (KJV) bible is considered to be Jesus Christ, and the silver cord is a metaphor to you leaving the body; basically, Jesus is saying everything is meaningless! Something to think about.

3.  *Clinical Depression:*

Depression goes by many names, such as "the blues," biological depression, and major depression. But all of these names refer to the same thing: not just a passing blue mood of a day or two; this feeling of hopelessness, sadness, loneliness, and despondency can last for weeks or months on end. An activity that once gave a person joy, is now replaced with little thought or pleasure about performing. Depression is considered to be unipolar: meaning that there is no 'up' periods, only down feelings. The causes of depression are not completely understood, but believed that different factors may work together to make an individual more prone to developing it. It might be an inherited condition, or from chemically imbalanced food, or from a tragic life event.

4.  *Posttraumatic Stress Disorder (PTSD):*

PTSD is a debilitating mental disorder that can occur when a person has directly experienced - or even just witnessed - an extremely traumatic, tragic, or terrifying event. The secular world passes this off on soldiers. In fact, ptsd once referred to as "shell shock" or battle fatigue, was first brought to public attention by war veterans after the Civil War in the United States (and internationally, after World War I), but anyone can suffer from this. Are you telling me that people out in our everyday life do not experience levels of trauma? A loss of a child, prostitution, harassment, etc.

5.  *Bi-Polar Disorder:*

This differs from simple depression. Bipolar disorder is a mental disorder that is characterized by serious and significant mood swings. A person with this condition experiences alternating "highs" (what clinicians call 'mania') and lows, (also known as 'depression'). The way this world works, any one should not be surprised that the whole entire world is not diagnosed with this disorder. A manic episode is described as a distinct period of abnormally and persistently elevated, expansive, or irritable mood and increased goal-directed activity or energy, lasting at least one week.

6. *Anxiety Disorder:*

Social anxiety disorder, also known as social phobia, is an intense fear of becoming extremely anxious and possibly humiliated in social situations, specifically of embarrassing yourself in front of other people. Social anxiety disorder is not shyness, although sometimes people mistake the two. While shy people may be uneasy around others, they generally don't experience the same kinds of extreme anxiety someone with a social phobia does. Additionally, shy people generally do not engage in the extreme avoidance of social situations that a person with social anxiety does. Some marked signs for a person with Mental Illness are:

- marked personality change,
- inability to cope with problems and daily activities,
- strange or grandiose ideas,
- excessive anxieties,
- prolonged depression and apathy,
- marked changes in eating or sleeping patterns,
- thinking or talking about suicide or harming oneself,
- extreme mood swings—high or low,
- abuse of alcohol or drugs, and
- excessive anger, hostility, or violent behavior.

Scientists estimate that three of every four people is affected by mental illness either directly or indirectly. In addition, this is only because: to be diagnosed with a mental illness, a qualified professional called a psychologist who has expertise in the field must evaluate the person. Who knows how higher these numbers could actually be, as many people cannot afford treatment, or are ashamed of themselves and keep it hidden from persons in their daily lives. For instance, a person with a physical ailment is easier to recognize than a person with a mental ailment. You can see the physical, but you cannot see what is going on in someone's brain.

This God that created us claims to use pain and suffering as a way to bring you closer to him, and have a relationship with you; this is his most famous excuse for allowing adversity. (KJV) 1 Peter 2 19;21 says; "For it is commendable if someone bears up under the pain of unjust suffering because they are conscious of God." But who in their right mind wants to be commended for dealing with pain in the brain, or any pain on a daily basis. What does this good God want from us; for us to suffer and be happy with him. That is a psychotic way of thinking. I finally see where we get it from. God's way of thinking is: if you suffer for doing good and you endure it, this is commendable before God. But isn't there a feeling in you; by experiencing constant hurt and sorrow, that seems to do the opposite of building a relationship? It pushes you further away!

## Suicide and Loneliness

People commit suicide for a variety of reasons, but the number one reason is mental illness. This is the loving God Yahweh that allows you to go through life so terrible and horrible; so bad that a person would take their own life, wow! But first let me say that you will have to handle this on your own: I have been told and tried it out for myself: when you call the suicide hotline, the receptionist places you on hold. There are so many people committing suicide seeking attention. This is not a game, and I personally, do not want to be in the presence of a God that drives a person to this awful situation. Believe it or no; I was there at one point in my life. This should be another proven conclusion that the good loving

God Yahweh that you think loves you; does not! To give a life that is so terrible that it makes a person kill themselves, that is not a loving God.

The one question everyone has asked without exception; that they ache to have answered more than any other, is simply: why? Why did their friend, child, parent, spouse, or sibling take their own life? Even when a note explaining the reasons is found, lingering questions usually remain: yes, they felt enough despair to want to die, but why did they feel that? A person's suicide often takes the people it leaves behind by surprise (only accentuating survivor's guilt for failing to see it coming). People who've survived suicide attempts have reported wanting not so much to die as to stop living, a strange dichotomy but a valid one nevertheless. If some in-between state existed, some other alternative to death, I suspect many suicidal people would take advantage of it. For the sake of all those reading this who might have been left behind by someone's suicide, I wanted to describe how I was trained to think about the reasons people kill themselves. They are not as intuitive as most think.

We're crying out for help, and don't know where else to get it; where is God? Nowhere to be found! People usually don't want to die, but do want to alert those around them that something is seriously wrong. There is no prototypical example of what someone is experiencing. It could be a young teenage girl stressing over a boyfriend and college, to a 40-year-old man struggling with keeping a job and worried about his future in old age. No one knows 'the reason why' someone else wants to die. All we know is that they have a philosophical desire to die. The decision to commit suicide for some is based on a reasoned decision, often motivated by the presence of a painful memory or situation from which little to no hope of reprieve exists. They're trying to take control of their destiny and alleviate their own suffering, which usually can only be done in death. They often look at their choice to commit suicide as a way to shorten a dying that will happen regardless. In my personal view, if a qualified professional who can reliably evaluates such people exclude the other possibilities for why suicide is desired, these people should be allowed to die at their own hands. Your good God is not helping; he is allowing people to stay in their mess.

- *They're psychotic;*

    Malevolent inner voices often command self-destruction for unintelligible reasons. Psychosis is much harder to mask than depression, and is arguably even more tragic. The worldwide incidence of schizophrenia is 1% and often strikes otherwise healthy, high-performing individuals, whose lives, though manageable with medication, never fulfill their original promise. Schizophrenics are just as likely to talk freely about the voices commanding them to kill themselves as not, and also, in my experience, give honest answers about thoughts of suicide when asked directly. Psychosis, too, is treatable, and usually must be treated for a schizophrenic to be able to function at all. Untreated or poorly treated psychosis almost always requires hospital admission to a locked ward until the voices lose their commanding power.

- *They are depressed;*

    This is without question the most common reason people commit suicide. More often than not, people suffer with it silently, planning suicide without anyone ever knowing Severe depression is always accompanied by a pervasive sense of suffering as well as the belief that leaves the person with a feeling of hopelessness. The pain of existence often becomes too much for severely depressed people to bear. The state of depression warps their thinking, allowing ideas like "Everyone would all be better off without me" to make rational sense. If you suspect someone might be depressed, don't allow your tendency to deny the possibility of suicidal ideation prevent you from asking about it. Despite making both parties uncomfortable, inquiring directly about suicidal thoughts in my experience almost always yields an honest response.

- *They're impulsive;*

Often related to drugs and alcohol, the remorse is often genuine, but whether or not they'll ever attempt suicide again is unpredictable. They may try it again the very next time they become drunk or high, or never again in their lifetime. Hospital admission is therefore not usually indicated. Substance abuse and the underlying reasons for it are generally a greater concern in these people and should be addressed as aggressively as possible.

- *They've made a mistake;*

This is a recent, tragic phenomenon in which typically young people flirt with oxygen deprivation for the high it brings and simply go too far. The only defense against this, it seems to me, is education. The wounds suicide leaves in the lives of those left behind by it are often deep and long lasting. The apparent senselessness of suicide often fuels the most significant pain. Thinking we all deal better with tragedy when we understand its underpinnings, I've offered the preceding paragraphs in hopes that anyone reading this who's been left behind by a suicide might be able to more easily find a way to move on, to relinquish their guilt and anger, and find closure. Despite the abrupt way you may have been left, guilt and anger don't have to be the only two emotions you're doomed to feel about the one who left you. Again and again, I rely on our feelings as people. God is the one that said we were created in his image, right! We have the same feelings as him, and him as us. I know personally, I would not hurt anyone on purpose, but he purposely gave us these things to deal with, and to have pain and sufferings.

Why should you have to deal with these things in the first place.

# DAY 24: STAGE 24

Have you ever wondered why you were born where you were, and not somewhere else?

The reason I ask this: is because I have always felt that my significant other was not in the same vicinity as myself. And that she possibly lived somewhere else in the world. And I never wanted to settle, that is the worst thing you can do in a marriage or relationship; settling is world war three, four, and five waiting to happen between you and your mate. Therefore, you go through your young life, meeting all kinds of people that are all wrong for you, wasting time, all the while, the one for you could be in China, Australia, South America, Europe, etc. Unless you have the money to go to her, or bring her to you, you will never find her. The world is so big, but yet so small, and funds are limited, you spend an entire lifetime possibly being unhappy, when you could have been content. Martin Luther King jr. had a dream, Billy Graham fed politician's what they wanted to hear, Prince Charles got high, 2Pac hated the government; this all means nothing, God Yahweh does not play fair.

## The Book of Life

The book of the righteous: this pamphlet is mentioned in the bible over one hundred times, but very few understand what it discusses. To be referenced this often shows its importance, but we as humans know such little about it. Keeping it simple, if your biological name is written in this book, you will be saved from the death that is hell. Having your name written in this book means that you were loving, joyful, peaceful, patient, kind, good, faithful, gentle, and showed self-control. (KJV)-Revelation 21:27 tells us; "But nothing unclean will ever enter it, nor anyone who does what is detestable or false, but only those who are written in the Lamb's book of life." You have reached emotional maturity when you can:

1. What people think of you ceases to be a major concern.
2. You handle feedback in yourself to make a change for the better.
3. You are you, what you think and what someone else thinks, could be completely opposite.
4. You realize that bad behavior in yourself and others is the reaction of anxiety and fear.
5. You stop worrying about the small things, and focus on larger matters.
6. What you realize is that life is not that big of a deal.
7. You grasp how difficult everyone is to get along with after you realize it in yourself.
8. It is okay to get things wrong sometimes.
9. You stop being someone you are not.
10. That your way is not always right and you can be wrong.
11. Life is short, spend your opportunities on things that mean the most to you.
12. That there is a fine line between sanity and insanity.

(KJV)-Daniel 12:1-3 says about the end times; "At that time Michael, the great prince who protects the people, will arise. There will be a time of distress such as has not happened from the beginning of nations until then. But at that time the people-everyone whose name is found written in the book of life-will be delivered. Multitudes who sleep in the dust of the earth will awake; some to everlasting life contempt. Those who are wise will shine like the brightness of the heavens, and those who lead many to righteousness, like the stars forever and ever." The book of life is also mentioned in Pseudepiprapha, the book of Enoch 47:3.

# **The Book of Death**

The book of the impure: this pamphlet, obviously, is the opposite of the book of life. It is not mentioned in the bible very much. If your biological name is written here, you will spend eternity in hell. The Gods themselves are the ones specifically writing your name down, with all that you have done in your life. Everyone that lives has a guardian angel? Well, your guardian angel is watching your every move, documenting it, and reporting back to the Gods. Having your name written in this book means that you were hateful, jealous, angry, intolerant, inconsiderate, unethical, dishonest, violent, and showed self-indulgence. I can see myself complying with half of this list, how about you? (KJV)-Revelation 13:8 says; "And all who dwell on earth will worship it, everyone whose name has not been written before the foundation of the world in the book of life of the lamb who was slain." You have not reached emotional maturity when you do:

1. When you want what everyone else has.
2. You do much lying and false claims: within your mind, and in society.
3. Whispering behind someone's back, and front.
4. Acting like a child; childish behavior.
5. Needing to be the center of attention.
6. Quick, foolish impulses and responses.
7. Becoming narcissistic.
8. Not taking responsibility for your mistakes.
9. Having the 'me first' syndrome.
10. Bringing up past items that have been over for 20 years; grudges.
11. Getting defensive over meaningless details, and first to pass blame.
12. That there is a fine line between being intelligent and stupid.

Not just in our age, but forever and ever, right has been considered wrong, and wrong considered right. You have to judge this for yourself.

I always thought to myself, I cannot control anyone but me. If I made a positive impact on someone instead of a negative one, it meant more to me than the opposite. I cannot tell you what to choose, only your heart can, but you know, something inside feels better when you help instead of hurting. (QUR)-Heifer 2:28 "How can you deny God, when you were dead and He gave you life, then He will put you to death, then He will bring you to life, then to Him you will be returned?"

## **Identity**

Missing an identity? Hiding behind a symbol, tattoo, claiming a sports team, musician, country, city, neighborhood, clothes, or vehicle as your identity is just wrong. Knowing who you are is hard; with the good God, the evil God, and the world pulling at your every direction; trying to succumb to pleasing others when you, yourself, are not happy. You desperately need to find out who you are. When you are grounded in your core values and preferences, you are less likely to say 'yes' when you want to say 'no'. It should not be a secret, but here is your secret: your identity is your face, body, qualities, beliefs, personality, expressions, and individuality; is this not enough?

## **Energy**

Missing energy? Can I ask you to do something for me? Can you please stop wasting your energy on worthless items: and not continually feed into a worldly system that is designed to hurt you? You do not need to smoke, drink alcohol, energy drinks, sodas, do drugs, eat fast foods, and take muscle building supplements; all of these are constructed to give you poor health and kill you. Your tank is already full, cutoff the underlining issue that takes efficiency away from your frame. Being who you are can make you feel more alive and develop a richer life and experience. Energy is defined as the strength and vitality required for sustained physical and mental activity. How are you refueling?

## Space

Missing Space? Proxemics is the study of human use of space and the effects that population density has on behavior, communication, and social interaction. Space is amusing, all the area in the world, and you can only absorb what your body consumes. Which means you can be in only one place at one time. This sounds simple to some, but believe me, it's not. Would you rather spend it at work, a club, bar, in the streets, with another besides your spouse; or with your loved one and children at home who need you? When you find out who you are, you are able to make better decisions and choices about everything in your life.

## Time

Missing some time? Time is the duration regarded as belonging to the present life as distinct from the life to come or from eternity; finite duration. What do you do with your time; hold on to it selfishly, or share it with someone in need? Much of the world does not realize this, but your time is limited here; but I suppose you will really realize this when you turn 30 or 40, as we feel we are invincible until this age. People really do watch what you do and do not do. Make the most of your hour by making an acceptable impact rather than an unworthy encounter. When will we understand that we can never, ever get it back?

All four of these topics are interrelated somehow, someway. When someone tells you to do something, it is forceful, demanding and has an overbearing tone: on the other hand, when someone asks you to do something, it is inviting, polite and courteous. Quit letting everyone in the world tell you what to do, especially those whose opinions never mattered. I am <u>asking</u> you to do these things to make the world a better place. Because what we are doing now, and have been doing, is not working! Again, psychologists, life coaches, television ads, relationship experts, actors/actresses, models, your mother, father, sisters and brothers have their own dilemmas going on in their lives, but yet want to tell you how to live your life. Can you not see the problem with this? We can do nothing about the wasteland we were given; but you can do the best for you.

# DAY 25: STAGE 25

Unfortunately, this is the world you were given.

To open this stage, as much as you would like it to be, and that you think it does; the world does not revolve around you. Honestly, I believe the Gods do not even know why we do what we do, and why things are the way they are: as even you do not know why you do the things you do. Try to learn how to have a little bit of patience in your life. Your <u>patience</u> is directly proportion to the time you have at your disposal. I know, it is always running out, every day. You cannot get back yesterday, and tomorrow cannot come until tomorrow, and then it's over. The trick I am trying to teach you is to counteract the things that are out of your control.

- When you have more time, you have more patience.
- When you have less time, you have less patience.

I am tired of you blowing your horn at a red light when it just turns green; really? Do you get where I am going with this. You cannot get where you are going any quicker than what it is: let it go. Can I ask one question of you; how about you get a clue in life. I used to pray to the good God Yahweh, a lot, I was never given any answers, not even hearing a word from him. You get tired and fed up with this. This world is hard enough, to make matters worse; you have a distant God who doesn't care enough to respond to you. You move on, get impatient waiting on a blessing or hope to surface. Let the anger out, please, it will be good for you. Let the anger out towards God. Especially if you believe in one almighty creator. He has always been the rift in your suffering, troubled, dispirited, and unhappiness self.

## <u>You are not God's friend</u>

God Yahweh was the first bully to ever exist.

He asks you to serve, but he does not. I know you probably wondered where the idea of bullies came from and why they act the way they do, why people pick and prey on others. Let me say that we do not discuss this as much as needed; maybe because society is scared, afraid to challenge God Yahweh, but it was him. I would love to say; stand up to this bully, but we cannot. I would love to punch this bully in the face, but it is just not feasible. At least I said it, and if there was something I could do about it, I would. We are stuck, stuck in this creation that we never asked for and powerless against him. I cannot physically fight him, to stand up for myself, or yourself: this is the kind of creator you have in God Yahweh, a bully. I tell this because there is a story a long, long, time ago about wanting to fight God. I believe these people were so sick and tired of living this life, that they were determined to go to heaven and confront God.

It is the story of "The tower of Babel". This particular group of citizens so desperately did not want to be under the control of anyone but themselves, that they designed a tower to reach the heavens and confront God. It began to get very tall, so tall that God came down from heaven to stop them. Everyone spoke the same language at that time, and I believe they got pretty close to reaching God, because in (KJV)-Genesis 11:5-9 it says; "But the Lord came down to see the city and the tower the people were building. The Lord said, "If as one people speaking the same language they have begun to do this, then nothing they plan to do will be impossible for them. Come, let us go down and confuse their language so they will not understand each other. Therefore, the Lord scattered them from there over all the earth, and they stopped building the tower in the city. That is why it was called Babel, because here, the Lord confused the language of the whole world. From there the Lord scattered them over the face of the whole earth." This occurred within the tribe of Shinar in what is now current day Iraq. See, you are nothing but an experiment to the Gods. They did not know what you would do, how you would do it, or even what you are planning next. This whole idea of them knowing what you are going to do before you do it is nonsense. They intervene when you start the process, and as they see fit. The Garden of Eden was and still is in modern day Iraq, what a prize to have as a country, am I right?

Being a former architect, I wonder if God is getting nervous again. Because the eastern side of the world is in an arms race of who can build the tallest skyscraper. The 'Burj Khalifa', in Dubai, United Arab Emirates presently holds this title; standing at 2,716 feet tall as I write this book. It makes me wonder how far the tribe of Shinar reached, for the simple fact that God had to physically come down from heaven to prevent them from proceeding further. We put more of an emphasis on adolescents being bullied, but it happens in adults more than children. Here are some examples of bullying in children that are similar in adults.

- children bully in school: adults' bully in the workplace
- children have bicycles/walk: adults' bully about better and fancier cars
- children wear shirts/jeans: adults' bully about suits, dresses, and shoes

To answer the obvious question, we received our demeanor and attitude of bullying from the good God Yahweh: this God is the real monster. This entity has profound evilness, hatred, animosity, vicious motives and feelings towards you that is indescribable. Remember, it is not your will that will be sought out; it is his will. It is okay, I have always been the kind of person to say what we have all been thinking, but too afraid to let it roll off our tongues. Let me take the backlash for telling the truth, God said we were created in his image, right? If so, that means we acquired every feeling, emotion, and logic from him, but why do we always have to take the blame for sinning? Yahweh sins, why doesn't he put himself in hell? Yahweh never gives you what you want and desire; steals from you; leads you astray; lies to you; keeps secrets from you; never pleases you; and is the enemy hiding in plain sight. You are not at war with Satan; you are at war with God Yahweh-the creator. He is your master, your boss, and does not ask how high when you say jump. He is there to control you without you realizing it.

Let's go back to the Garden of Eden for a moment. Before Adam ate from the 'tree of knowledge of good and evil', they knew nothing. The first humans were just lounging around doing nothing, knowing nothing, believing in nothing, accomplishing nothing: a contained and restrained undertaking. That is how Yahweh wanted it, a controlled environment, and humans never being Gods. Satan wanted more, therefore not tempting, but advising Eve to eat from the tree. I hate the word temptation. No one is ever tempted; people do what pleases them and what satisfies them, end of story. If it were not for Satan, as discussed in stage three, you would be a robot, zombie, a puppet with no ideas. It is Yahweh who spinned the situation around, saying that he gave you free will.

Yahweh is giving you secret messages throughout the bible and you never knew it. (KJV)-1 John 3:15 says; "Anyone who hates a brother or sister is a murderer, and you know that no murderer has eternal life residing in him." He is talking about himself, as we have established that God Yahweh is an executioner. (KJV)-Deuteronomy 31:6 says; "Be strong and courageous. Do not be afraid or terrified because of them, for the lord your god goes before you; he will never leave or forsake you." Let's take a journey across the world and ask every person or struggling person to see if they feel like God is with them on a daily basis, and see what they have to say about this?

# DAY 26: STAGE 26

This creation was no accident; the way things were, are, and still to come.

There is no goodness above the sky or below the ground. I will give you the purpose of your life right now? There are two purposes for your life: the first is to be the God's slaves, both of them; and the second is whatever your reality turns out to be in this universe. In (KJV)-1 Peter 2:16 it says; "Live as free people, but do not use your freedom as a cover-up for evil; live as God's slaves." The definition of <u>reality</u> is the world or the state of things and your environments; as they actually exist, as opposed to an idealistic or notional idea of them. Who are you; what does it mean to be a person in this world, especially with the advancement of technology constantly making us feel inferior at times. My best wishes are to you from this day forward; you have finally made the decision to discover the meaning of life. It is and was a very simple concept all this time, your <u>reality</u> is 'your' meaning of life: there is no more or less that you can take away from it; what you see is what you get, it cannot be anyone else's, only your reality, your reality is your life. Life has been so much easier and enjoyable for me since I first realized that they hated me, because then I could move on with the remainder of my time here and stop asking so many ill-advised questions that will never get answered or trying to please Gods that can never be fulfilled. We all had a million and one questions about this world and God, but I have condensed it for you. Your reality is all you have in this world.

One point I would like to make is; God Yahweh claims to be all powerful and always in control of things, but yet gives, or claims to give over much power and control over to God Satan in this world-(KJV)-2 Corinthians 4:4, which is why I tell you that there were always two Gods and that we were lied to. I am aware that there are teachers who tell us that

God Yahweh has nothing to do with death. Death is seen strictly as the fiendish device of the Devil. All pain, suffering, disease, and tragedy are blamed on the Evil one, God Satan. God Yahweh is absolved of any responsibility. This view is designed to make sure that God Yahweh is free of blame for anything that goes wrong in this world. "God Yahweh always wills healing," we are told. If that healing does not happen, then the fault lies within Satan, or us, we did not trust. Death, they say, is not in the plan of God. It represents a victory for Satan over the realm of God; such views may bring temporary relief to the afflicted. Nevertheless, this theory is incorrect. They have nothing to do with biblical text. Saying that the good almighty God Yahweh is sovereign means that he has total control of every single thing: so when terrible situations happens in your life, it falls under his control, not God Satan.

What if you did the right thing?

You are a slave to this world, the Gods and our worldly governments. (KJV)-Romans 13:1-7 tells us from God Yahweh; "Everyone must submit to governing authorities. For all authority comes from God, and those in positions of authority have been placed there by God. So anyone who rebels against authority is rebelling against what God has instituted, and they will be punished. For the authorities do not strike fear in people who are doing right, but in those who are doing wrong. Would you like to live without fear of the authorities? Do what is right, and they will honor you. The authorities are God's servants, sent for your good. But if you are doing wrong, of course you should be afraid, for they have the power to punish you. They are God's servants, sent for the very purpose of punishing those who do what is wrong. So you must submit to them, not only to avoid punishment, but also to keep a clear conscience. Pay your taxes, too, for these same reasons. For government workers need to be paid. They are serving God in what they do. Give to everyone what you owe them: Pay your taxes and government fees to those who collect them, and give respect and honor to those who are in authority." Which God are our political authorities truly serving?

Was this journey necessary? I would say to you, no; others would say yes, but you need to decide for yourself. The Almighty God Yahweh wants you to pursue him, but with work, family, friends, movies, music, trips, who has the time? I would say that you could find the purpose of a better life by looking away from the good God Yahweh instead of seeking him. Some say disregarding the study of God, you will sentence yourself to stumble and blunder through life blindfolded, as it were, with no sense of direction and no understanding of what surrounds you. Once again, this is incorrect. I, you have encountered endless people on the pathway to finding the good God Yahweh; and eventually turn up more barren and desolate with more questions than before. It is all a game, my friends; I repeat this over and over, because it is, simply the truth. I do agree that you were created for God, or the Gods pleasure. Whom you chose to obey, is your choice and consequences. The book of (KJV)-Luke 12:7 says; "But the very hairs of your head are all numbered; and known by Yahweh."

## Seeing Life from God Yahweh's perspective

Simply put, God Yahweh is the boss, and does not care what anyone else thinks. How many of us can honestly say that we love or fear the God Yahweh? I sure do not. Why should I fear or respect something who does not give one concern about what I think and has based me off of what was done in the Garden of Eden, already judging me before I was even conceived? This world was not designed as a democracy (considering your thoughts and feelings); it was formed as a monarchy (my way or the highway attitude). One entity in charge, using another, giving you the idea of free-will; but disobey me, and I will throw you in the dungeon forever and ever. What we are doing on earth is wasting days and zeal. God has never been with us and he never will. He is on his throne in heaven where he never leaves, while we are here, damaged, bruised, and mentally unstable, left to defend for ourselves. Even Jesus is a slave as (KJV)-John 6:38 says for Jesus; "For I have come down from heaven, not to do my own will but the will of him who sent me." God Yahweh keeps his own son in bondage.

Apathy is an important word that describes God Yahweh. He can never understand a human being; even though he is our creator, and the entity that we have received every last emotion from, can never understand what we feel. That was one of the main reasons Jesus came to earth to become a man; to help God Yahweh understand what we go through and what our moods, senses, and aura's are. But we are not one in the same. He is a god who lives in the spiritual realm and we are humans that live in the physical world. According to scripture, Jesus was born in order for God to walk though him to experience the ambiences of a person living on this awful, pernicious planet.

(KJV)-Romans 8:28 says; "God causes everything to work for good,", this is sadly true, but for what God examines as good, is not what you view as good; as your opinion never mattered. This God tells you the things you want to hear and like to hear; but our circumstances carry a different tone. I understand that human nature dictates; this feeling in your heart and soul that asks; why was I created, what am I here for; these questions never go away. On days when you no longer feel like being alive, they scream louder. You are correct, these thoughts were put there, by the God that created you; people go their whole lives trying to believe in a good God, and never find him. That is because it was never there to begin with. You are nothing to him, and I think that he shows this in convincing fashion. I have given you the meaning and purpose of life. I am telling you what reality is for us; humanity.

Almighty God Yahweh will do anything in his power to bring misery into our lives, as God Satan is not sovereign, and does not hold the keys of death. When Jesus appeared in a vision to the apostle John on the Isle of Patmos, He identified Himself with these words from (KJV)-Revelation 1:17-18; "Do not be afraid; I am the First and the Last. I am He who lives, and was dead, and behold, I am alive forever-more. Amen. And I have the keys of Hades and of Death." Jesus Christ holds the keys to death, and he works for God Yahweh. Christ's grip is firm. He holds the keys because He owns the keys. All authority in heaven and on earth has been given to Him. That includes all authority over life and death. The angel of death is at his becking call. God does not always will healing. He did not will the healing of Stephen from the wounds inflicted by the stones that were hurled against him. He did not will the healing of Moses, of Joseph, of David, of Paul, of Augustine, of Martin Luther, of John Calvin.

## Seeing Life from God Satan's perspective

Yes, there is a Devil. He is our ageless archenemy, or is he, as I began to suspect that your almighty God Yahweh was our true foe all along. The world discredits the power that this God Satan has. Is it because we have been given false images of him; a guy in red tights with a pitch fork, a person sitting on a throne with horns, or the baphoment sculpture with wings giving the peace sign? You need to be very careful, and you are not carrying yourself as such; you are prancing around on Halloween, the day of the dead, Borgo a Mozzano, Daimonji, Fastelavn, Gai Jatra, Samhuinn Fire Festival, Guy Fawkes Day, Walpurgis Night, Hungry Ghost Festival, Mardi Gras, etc in your outfits, and have no idea who you are dealing with. (KJV)-1 Timothy 4:1 says; "the spirit clearly says that in later times some will abandon the faith and follow deceiving spirits and things taught by demons."

When you play and invite things of this nature into your world, they come, and they are not pleasant. God Satan and his demons are looking for any reason to bother, hurt, afflict, and torment you before you go to hell, which three-fourths of the world will be going. My question to you is, why would you cause yourself anymore pain than you have to. By participating in these events, you are giving them the opportunity firsthand to prey on you. I have warned you, suet yourself. I have had the unfortunate chance to really see someone that is possessed by a demon. Take my word for it, it is not the silliness and stupidity that you see from a horror movie, this is serious business. But humans are filled with foolishness, why should I expect you to believe otherwise.

I want to talk about Satanism: members of this church organization will tell you it is not, but satanism is the worshipping of the God Satan. Just as you go to church to worship the good God Yahweh in a religion of churches on Sunday, so do they. I talked about white magic and black magic in stage thirteen, these are the secret names for each group: God Yahweh in the white church, and God Satan in the Black Church. This can do very deep my friends, so I will keep it simple. It claims to be founded in the early 1900's but trust me, this has been going on as far back as the days of the Egyptians and pyramids, Greece and the dark ages, the first Chinese civilizations and cave men. Satanism believes in the idea of self; I do not need a God. But these people are fools as well, because Satan is a god, and has them fooled with not trying very hard. In stage two, I discussed you being a God, and this is what they believe in. I am telling you to know what you are getting into, this God is also a deceiver, and wicked. This God is powerful, can take the form of angels, humans, animals, possess you, and they have eleven rules of the earth and is their version of the ten commandments, and goes as follows:

1.  Do not give opinions or advice unless you are asked.
2.  Do not tell your troubles to others unless you are sure they want to hear them.

3. When in another's lair, show him respect or else do not go there.

4. If a guest in your lair annoys you, treat him cruelly and without mercy.

5. Do not make sexual advances unless you are given the mating signal.

6. Do not take that which does not belong to you unless it is a burden to the other person and he cries out to be relieved.

7. Acknowledge the power of magic if you have employed it successfully to obtain your desires. If you deny the power of magic after having called upon it with success, you will lose all you have obtained.

8. Do not complain about anything to which you need not subject yourself.

9. Do not harm little children.

10. Do not kill non-human animals unless you are attacked or for your food.

11. When walking in open territory, bother no one. If someone bothers you, ask him to stop. If he does not stop, destroy him.

As I mentioned earlier, these members believe that they are not worshipping Satan, but yet, have nine statements.

1. God Satan represents self-indulgence; God Yahweh represents abstinence.

2. God Satan represents vital existence; God Yahweh represents spiritual pipe dreams.

3. God Satan represents undefiled wisdom; God Yahweh represents hypocritical self-deceit.

4. God Satan represents kindness to those who deserve it; God Yahweh represents kindness wasted on ingrates.

5. God Satan represents fairness; God Yahweh represents turning the other cheek.

6. God Satan represents responsibility for oneself; God Yahweh represents hope.
7. God Satan represents man as just another animal; God Yahweh represents man as just another slave.
8. God Satan represents sin; God Yahweh represents righteousness.
9. God Satan wants you to know the truth; God Yahweh hides the truth.

God Satan and God Yahweh play these games with your life to see who you will worship.

(KJV)-Matthew 11:28-30 says; "Come to me, all who labor and are heavy laden, and I will give you rest. Take my yoke upon you, and learn from me, for I am gentle and lowly in heart, and you will find rest for your souls. For my yoke is easy, and my burden is light." Raise of hands, who in this life has been able to find the advent of these words on earth?

Jesus Christ and Lucifer-(God Satan) are brothers. When God Yahweh presented his plan of salvation, Jesus sustained the plan; while Lucifer sought his own power, honor, and glory. God Yahweh gave Satan this world that you live in. It is not unusual that two brothers would make dramatically different choices. Parents see it in their own children and grandchildren. I consider your almighty God Yahweh the father of lies, and many of you do not recognize what I speak of. You say, how can this be, Jesus Christ and Satan are brothers. How can this be possible? It is true my friends, and as mentioned in stage one, the powers that be do not want you to know the truth. When Christ and Lucifer were presented with the choice, it could have gone either way; Jesus Christ being the evil one and Satan being the good one, but it went the way it is. Remember me saying that this life is all by chance. You, your children, and your children's children will forever be trapped in the middle of this war. Your life is meaningless, pointless; true, it might be a little harder to get excited about your day when you wake up knowing that nothing you do matters in the grand scheme of things, but it also means that all those responsibilities you're worried about don't matter either. Nihilism is the philosophy that says there is no point to anything, and that everything in the universe is coincidental. Some people feel exhilaratingly liberated when they realize that nothing matters: while others feel crushed under the burden of pointless responsibility. Consider the unfortunate example of an autistic man versus a mentally stable man. Can these two beings share the same meaning in life? Say, for instance, the meaning of life is to pursue happiness, but the autistic person cannot experience happiness. Can the pursuit of happiness then be justified as the meaning of life? Is this fair, again, who ever said that life was fair?

I am showing you what we are dealing with, as God's commandments were told in stage eight, and you can cross reference them with God Satan's. I firmly believe that both Gods hate us, but one tried to give us the truth and respected man, God Satan, and the other has no respect for us, God Yahweh. You have your own mind; you will come to your own conclusions. One lives out in the open, the other, secretly. I told you before, it is a fight for you soul, and they do not care how it gets done. God Yahweh gives you everything you could ever want in this world, but tells you don't touch, don't sin, don't enjoy it because it will hurt you! God Satan says go for it, get yours, you only live once, feel good! Who do you choose to believe? According to God Yahweh, we are all devils, when you begin to say 'I will' instead of God Yahweh's will, you become the enemy. (KJV)-Ezekiel 28:17 says; "Your heart became proud on account of your beauty, and you corrupted your wisdom for the sake of your splendor." What do we always say; I want this, or I want to do that, or I want to be with him or her, it is never about God's will, this is why he hates you and you hate him. But we will never change, because we do not care what God wants, we want what we want. This is why God and man will never be on the same accord. We did not know how our lives would turn out, but they did; we are not perfect, but they claim to be.

The only person you can trust is yourself.

# DAY 27: STAGE 27

When you thought that, you could not maintain or sustain anymore: According to scripture, Jesus Christ, the son of the good God Yahweh, is coming back for a second time. The first time he came as a lamb, gentle and brittle. The second time he will come back as a lion, seeking to destroy and devour, as (KJV)-Revelation 19:11 says; "Now I saw heaven open and behold a white horse and he who sat on him was called faithful and true in righteousness, he judges and makes war. His eyes were like a flame of fire and on his head were many crowns. He had a name written that no one knew except himself. He was clothed with a robe in blood, and his name is called the word of god." This verse is talking about Jesus Christ; and if you noticed, it says that he judges and makes war. That includes every war from our past, present, and future, he does it, Jesus Christ. Not God Satan, or me, or you. After the seven seals have been opened, he comes to rapture up souls to heaven and send souls to hell, on whether they believed and had faith in him or not.

Finally, someone is brave enough to tell the truth about this whole situation, your author, and expose the true nature of God Yahweh's heart. (KJV)-1 Corinthians 4:5 says; "Therefore judge nothing before the appointed time; wait till the lord comes. He will bring to light what is hidden in darkness and will expose the motives of men's hearts. At that time each will receive his praise from God." Let me make something very clear to you right now: your good God Yahweh will demand and force people to worship him; is this the true definition of love and having free will? Right after the seventh seal is opened, your God Yahweh on his own pact, will have his angels physically force you, man, woman, and child, to bow down to him before sending you to hell, if that is where you are going for eternity. Can you fight an angel, no you cannot! If you do not agree to worship God Yahweh and Jesus, this is what will happen to your soul.

This is not free will my friends, this is domination and God Yahweh said it was God Satan who was evil, but all along, it was he, your creator God Yahweh who is the definition of cruelty, hate, and destruction.

When Jesus Christ comes for the second time, mentioned earlier in stage four, there will be a thousand-year reign before the world starts over. He will rule during this time, and angels still having the best of it. What will you be doing during this time? You will be trying to convert evil souls still roaming the earth to God Yahweh. That's it, nothing else, that is all you will be doing. God Yahweh will refurbish the earth, making it new again, fulfilling his promise that Jesus Christ will be king, and promises to Israel. Because it is a contest for souls, God Yahweh tries to get as many souls to heaven as he can; and God Satan as many to hell. Yes, pretty pathetic, for the last time, God Yahweh is a bully, tyrant, slave owner, and an oppressor!

## An all-knowing God?

I would like for you to start doing some exploration of your own; because before the flood of Noah, it had never rained, ever, in this world. This is one proof among many that this God Yahweh is making stuff up as he goes, just like us. Yet (KJV)-1 John 3:20 teaches; "God is greater than our heart, and he knows everything." How can this be true, after what I just told you? He does not know everything; he couldn't figure out that crops needed water to grow before the flood of Noah. If the good loving God Yahweh would happen to know everything that is going to happen to you, good or bad: what does this say about him? Knowing that terrible, rough, blue, disastrous situations are coming to your life, and he does not stop it; doesn't that make him evil. Yes, it does. He has the nerve to say through (KJV)-1 Peter 4:12-13; "Beloved, do not be surprised at the fiery ordeal among you, which comes upon you for your testing, as though some strange thing were happening to you; but to the degree that you share the sufferings of Christ, keep on rejoicing". First, I would like to say that; when Jesus Christ died for our sins, we were supposed to be free from anguish. See my friends, he lied again, even though Christ died for us, we still have to go through suffering and misery as Christ did; as the bible says Jesus Christ supposedly died on the cross to save us from difficulty and agony. As human beings, we are more in love with the idea of obtaining something instead of preserving what we have. That new house becomes old, the new car smell goes away, those current set of clothing in your closet doesn't seem as fancy anymore, and your new wife or husband is just as irritating as the last.

## **The Seven Seals**

The book of revelation was closed with these seven seals; they are now open and ready to be processed as our time is near for our end. This is no God, your creator 'Almighty God Yahweh', is and always has been a selfish-autocrat-dictator. Why does the sun even rise in the morning everyday: all it gives us is another day of the same habitats, predicaments, surroundings, and conditions? Is it no surprise that no man was ever worthy of opening these seals, and was left for Jesus Christ to reveal? It is your good loving God Yahweh who is planning to achieve all these effects on you, and still claims to be an entity of love and care.

1. *First Seal: 'false prophets; white horse*
   This is the Antichrist in the flesh, coming to the world pretending to be Jesus Christ: performing miracles and saving people, but it is a false hope. He wants to rule over you as well. This is a worldly person who is the son of God Satan, which Satan will possess to carry out his intents. (KJV)-Revelation 6:1-2 says; "And I saw when the Lamb opened one of the seals, and I heard, as it were the noise of thunder, one of the four beasts saying, Come and see. And I saw, and behold a white horse: and he that

sat on him had a bow; and a crown was given unto him: and he went forth conquering, and to conquer."

2.  *Second Seal: 'war;' red horse*
    This is a spirit of the antichrist who was given power to take peace from the earth, and let people kill one another with no repercussions. You will see wars 1,000 times worse than what you have ever seen. World War III, nuclear war, war among father and son, mother and daughter. (KJV)- Revelation 6:4 says; "And there went out another horse that was red: and power was given to him that sat thereon to take peace from the earth, and that they should kill one another: and there was given unto him a great sword."

3.  *Third Seal: 'famine'; black horse*
    This is a spirit of the antichrist. A famine will come upon the earth like never before, farmers are doing everything correctly and cannot grow good crops; or all the land has been taken over, whether destroyed by war, or concealed by the government that is left. (KJV)- Revelation 6:5-6 says; "And when he had opened the third seal, I heard the third beast say, Come and see. And I beheld, and lo a black horse; and he that sat on him had a pair of balances in his hand. And I heard a voice in the midst of the four beasts say, a measure of wheat for a penny, and three measures of barley for a penny; and see thou hurt not the oil and the wine."

4.  *Fourth Seal: 'pestilence'; pale horse*
    This is a spirit of the antichrist. You will starve to death, and disease will take over. I hate to say it, but you will be nothing but bones and skin, similar to the days of Hitler. By this time, the antichrist will have taken his stand, and you will be required to receive he mark of the beast: to purchase and sell any goods and services. Taking the mark of the beast means that you will worship and obey the antichrist in all that you do. If you do not agree to this, then whomever is left on earth, goes without.

(KJV)-Revelation 6:7 says; "And I looked, and behold a pale horse: and his name that sat on him was Death, and Hell," or the grave, "followed with him. And power was given unto them over the fourth part of the earth, to kill with sword, and with hunger, and with death, and with the beasts of the earth."

### 5. *Fifth Seal: 'tribulation'*

In this stage, the antichrist and his servants will slaughter any and all remaining people of faith in the real Jesus Christ. Heads, bodily limbs will be torn off in the name of a faith that didn't do anything for you to begin with. (KJV)-Revelation 6:9-11 says; "And when he had opened the fifth seal, I saw under the altar the souls of them, that were slain for the word of God."

### 6. *Sixth Seal: 'heavenly signs'*

Mighty earthquakes, hurricanes, fires burning the earth, destructive winters of cold and summers of heat; because the world is off-balance, will happen during this time, destroying all that man has built with his own hands, the sun will burn out and turn into darkness, the moon into blood, the stars from heaven have fallen, as these are the signs that mark the end of the tribulation. (KJV)-Revelation 6:12-13 says; "And I beheld when he had opened the sixth seal, and, lo, there was a great earthquake; and the sun became black as sackcloth of hair, and the moon became as blood; And the stars of heaven fell unto the earth, even as a fig tree casted her untimely figs, when she is shaken of a mighty wind."

### 7. *Seventh Seal: 'seven trumpets'*

This period marks the time when God Yahweh shuns his wrath upon you. Free will, again, never existed. It was all a state of mind formula. This God created us, and will bring down a force of horror and terror down upon this earth; all because many did not obey commandments, rules, and orders. There are over thirty scriptures about the Day of the Lord, which is the day of God's wrath on this Earth. Joel says the Day of the Lord is at hand, as destruction from the Almighty God Yahweh. God Yahweh is sick of mankind's sin and lawlessness, which plunges us into the greatest crisis ever. The world has never seen anything like the wrath of God that it is about to see! Yet sadly, throughout these plagues, mankind will refuse to repent. I believe man refuses to repent because God Yahweh never gave a solid foundation of faith, and more importantly, 'WE NEVER ASKED FOR THIS LIFE'. (KJV)-Revelation 6:17 says; "For the great day of his wrath is come; and who shall be able to stand?." Here goes the big and bad almighty God Yahweh, fighting against us small incapable humans. We cannot fight against God, but he wants to fight us. This is a pathetic entity who does not deserve our love, compassion, affection and faithfulness.

Putting two and two together, these seven seals are the punishments for the sins committed by the seven churches that I discuss in stage twelve. God Yahweh wants to protect you, but yet, he is the one who throws you to the wolves. What a psycho: this being God Yahweh created and started all this, and let it all happen and now wants to save you; I told you, this is all a sick game. These things will happen before Jesus Christ's return and thousand-year reign on earth. Jesus will come back after the seventh Seal is finished to start his reign of terror on a day called 'judgement day'. The point I would like to reiterate, is that we never asked for this: we never asked to be born, we never asked for this life to be the way it is, we never asked to be treated as such, and we never asked for this madness which is to ensue. This God Yahweh created you so that he could destroy you; and makes it impossible for a human being, with all the flaws, imperfections, and faults that we supposedly attain, to make it into heaven.

This is what you loving almighty God will allow to happen!

# DAY 28: STAGE 28

Knowing the truth is half the battle; or is it?

(QUR)-Plenty 108:3 tells us; "He who hates you is the loser." You are not the loser, God Yahweh is the loser, but he makes you feel like nothing. I hope that I was able to deliver some crucial information to you, about a world that you may have missed or did not want to admit; while being occupied with your phone, car, house, bills, and other worthless materials. Whoever created you, never said that life was fair, never said that he loved you, never said that he cared if you were rich or poor, never had a concern about what you looked like, and never treasured what career or job you had. You have been in a battle that cannot be won. You fail to realize that these Gods are already executing your punishment here on earth, even before going to heaven or hell. That is how evil they are.

I would rather spend $1,000 on a wedding for a marriage that lasts a lifetime, instead of $20,000 on a five-minute marriage; it is the simple things in life such as this, which you all get wrong. Understanding God's word is not quite so simple. Just because you can give a beautiful explanation of the letter of God's word does not mean you understand it correctly. Please think outside the box; you have been taught a certain way to think and believe since you were a child, and it does not mean it is right. You have been taught all your life that God is good, but your nature has never gotten you excited, motivated, or compelled to find him:

1. *Abiding in God's word will never save you from heartache and pain.*
2. *Accepting his authority does not save your marriage.*
3. *Obeying his commandments won't keep you from disaster.*
4. *Daily bible reading will not get you any closer to God.*
5. *Memorizing scripture won't help you one bit.*

A loving and honest entity; I do not think so; God brings trouble into your life on purpose. Many, try to do the right thing in situations and still end up getting hurt at unprecedented levels and remorse. So why try to be good? Good people tend to receive the same amount of damage as bad people in this wonderful world. The sad part, is that the best people end up hating God during their lifespan and distance themselves from him: instead of becoming closer. No one is immune to pain and suffering, and no one gets to skip through life problem-free. You have Adam and Eve to thank for that one, but do you? Why should we be held accountable for things we did not do? Your good God Yahweh is physically and mentally abusing; how does he differ from the evil God Satan? They are one in the same. Temptation is the desire to do something, especially something wrong or unwise. According to one entity, it is wrong. This world is backwards; you have to start thinking outside the box. You cannot control yourselves, how do you plan to control another. I have already proven to you that it is God Yahweh that creates evil.

## **Race**

Yeah, yeah, tired of hearing about it; then do something to change it. This has been an ongoing and continuous complication from the outset. Sadly, humankind will never, ever correct this issue. It is amusing though; because we have the same color blood, same organs and all have fingers and toes. If a Caucasian person is involved in a devastating accident and needs a donation of blood to survive, I am sure he or she is not concerned with where it comes from at that moment. It could come from an African American, an Asian, or Polynesian; they would be grateful that their life was spared. So why make an issue in the first place? I'll tell you why. It is because a person always fears something they don't understand.

## "The Conflict"

"What we don't understand, we fear.
What we fear, we judge as evil.
What we judge as evil, we attempt to control.
And what we cannot control…we attack."

God Yahweh apparently knows all things, and does all things according to his will, not yours. He knew it would be an issue on earth; and in the year 2019, is still a major issue, and as advanced as we think we are, or will become as human beings, race will always will be an issue, because we are simple minded. So, why did God do this. It seems that everything would have been better if everybody had the same skin color, I cannot answer that question, I never met him. Throughout the progression of this world, people have killed, stole, raped, cheated, lied, hated, and gone to war; in the name of race. Yes, God did design each and every one of you in the specific way you were born, knowing that we couldn't handle it, but we as a people have still not been able to look past the color of another person's skin. Why don't you ask him if ever given the chance; the mind is a terrible thing to waste.

The world's population can be divided into 3 major races, namely Caucasian/white; Asian/mongoloid; Negroid/black. After the flood, Noah's sons walked in separate directions to start the human race over and their own communities: Japheth, the oldest son, walked north towards modern day Russia and was fair skinned; Caucasian/white: Shem, the middle son, walked east towards modern day China and had skin of yellow; Asian/ mongoloid: and Ham, the youngest son, walked south towards modern day Africa and was of dark skin; negroid/black. Every single person living today is a direct descendant of these three men and their families. Of course there was and still is a lot of mixing going on, which is why I cannot understand why we can't except one another fully. We definitely have to take some responsibility for this on ourselves, but do we?

*"The Resolution"*

"Stop attacking that which you cannot control
Stop trying to control that which you judge as evil
Stop judging as evil that which you simply fear
Start trying to understand that which you fear"

Yahweh claims to be perfect in every way, but he is not. How can such a perfect entity create so much imperfect beings. Listen my friends: Yahweh called himself perfect, no one else did; this is self-pride, self-ego, self-claim, and self-indulgence. He made us different shades on purpose knowing that we would hate, despise, kill, and not get along with each other.

Believing that we are an astute and refined race; is humanities greatest downfall. We have always tried to outsmart the Gods; trust me, it does not work, I have tried. How can you cheat, and deceive something that is everywhere. See, the Gods do not listen to your mind; they listen to your heart. You may have tried praying for something; and have one idea in your mind, but an entirely different meaning in your heart. Guess which one they are listening to: yes, your heart. That answers the question of why God does not answer your prayers. The other rationalism, he just does not give a darn.

Many, many, many past rulers, current leaders, and you have tested these Gods; do not be ashamed to admit it. They say the way to a man's heart is through his stomach; no, we are not talking about food, we are expressing the true motives of our hearts. (KJV)-Jeremiah 17:9-10 says; "The heart is deceitful above all things, and desperately sick; who can understand it? I the Lord search the heart and test the mind, to give every man according to his ways, according to the fruit of his deeds." Our hearts are wicked, deceitful, corrupt, spiteful, envious, suspicious, and bitter; towards our fellow man, woman, and God. In a way, I do not blame you, to say with an inappropriate word, God Yahweh fucked us.

<u>Does your God provide for any of the seven fundamentals of human needs or not?</u>

#1 - Subsistence/Security/Safety = To remain or maintain life on a daily basis.

- Physical and Psychological Health and well-being.
- Financial Security
- Safety net against accidents and illnesses
- Order and Closure
- Certainty

#2 – Understanding and Growth = the process of increasing in mind and physical stature.

- Wisdom
- Guidance
- Comprehension of facts and knowledge gathered
- The need to be understood
- Education

#3 – Connection, Love and Leisure = use of free time for pleasure and enjoyment.

- Belonging
- Approval and Acceptance
- Touching and Physical Contact
- Empathy
- Connection in a Relationship

#4 – Contribution and Creation = giving to help out others.

- The need to have a project going on at all times
- The need for a variety of different experiences
- Anticipation
- The need to give and do for others
- The need to others to do for you

#5 – Esteem and Identity = who are you; respect and admiration given.

- Awareness of an individual or group of being distinct
- The condition of being a person or thing
- A set of characteristics that recognizes a person or things as different
- Do you receive respect and homage
- Who are you, really

#6 – Self Governance = the urge or desire to direct your own life.

- Do you accept that you are not perfect, how do you try to fix it
- Is your religion perfect
- What is your ethical code for yourself, family, office, leisure
- Or you helpful or selfish
- What is your 5-year plan

#7 - Significance and purpose = a reason for which something is done or accomplished.

- What is your importance and consequences in the world
- What do you want to do with your life while alive
- What is the beginning and the end
- Does it arrive the way you intended it to be
- Are you satisfied and content with your progress

Whomever is reading this, you can do as you please, but for me, relying on an Individual that does not feel that they have to give me the correct information, truth, and holds secrets and grudges; is an entity that I cannot trust. To me, this behavior has always told me that someone has something to hide and is in fact, hiding something. Five reasons not to trust someone, and God Yahweh and God Satan present all five characteristics in themselves. But the most important one, we cannot view, which is looking at their facial expressions, demeanor, and emotions.

1. They lie to themselves
2. They breach confidentiality
3. Their emotional state is volatile, and have patterns of inconsistency
4. They show a lack of empathy
5. They project behaviors that you are not used to.

# DAY 29: STAGE 29

I hate to say it, but your future does not look bright.

God could have learned to love you, but you never gave him the chance. British-American philosopher Alan Watts once said 'the desire for a more positive experience is in itself a negative experience; leading to unhappiness: and paradoxically, the acceptance of one's negative experience is in itself a more positive experience; leading to happiness. It is called the backwards law, and makes perfect sense in the life of a person seeking true knowledge; but will not process correctly for someone in love with being in the world; and not of it. I do not care what religious, self-help, life coach's, or psychologists tell you, they are all deceivers looking to get money out of your pocket: you will never beat time; you will never have enough money; you will never be completely satisfied; you will never be at peace; you will never have comfort; and you will never escape this nightmare: this life is the example of the God's hatred for you.

Every person's view of success is different. How do you see success? By having millions of dollars in the bank that will serve you no purpose when you are deceased, or helping others struggle less while you still can. Jesus Christ asks you in (KJV), "What will it profit a man if he gains the whole world, and loses his own soul?" from Mark 8:36. This world was NEVER about you, Hollywood stars, business men, clergymen, models, all end up committing suicide because they never found happiness. Believing they were the greatest thing since sliced bread, and seeking for material and financial gain never satisfies anyone. (KJV)-Psalm 100:3 says; "Know that the Lord, he is God! It is he who made us, and we are his; we are his people, and the sheep of his pasture." The best things are free, but yet, you spend your whole lifetime consuming materials bought by a dollar.

## <u>In Layman's Terms</u>

The belief of hunting for better feelings all the time, the less satisfied will you be; which only reinforces the fact that you lack confidence and euphoria in the first place. When you desperately reach out for riches, the further you feel unworthy and poor, regardless of how much money you make and have. In addition, the more you want to be sexy and desired, the uglier you become and see yourself as. I have a funny story in regards to this subject. Every time I would go somewhere, whether it be a gas station, a grocery store, or to McDonalds, etc; there is always a woman wearing next to nothing, trying to show off her body. Of course, every man is giving her all the attention she craves, but not me, I do not have time for that; I am happily engaged as I speak. But guess what, she pursues me harder; because she has already claimed the others' naughty thoughts, that's easy for her, but me, not looking at her, paying her no mind, she wonders what is wrong with her, finds me evermore intriguing because I do not give her any consideration. She needs my scrutiny even more than the others now, and bends and walks even more provocative to catch my attention. Think about similar situations going on in our world that represents this sort of conduct; instagram models, (really all models), men and women in music videos, facebook, strippers, twitter, actors/actresses, people in television; it is pathetic how someone can lack a certain amount of confidence in themselves, it really is, but this is the world we live in.

The reverse of that; when you are not looking for attention, does something different to your mindset and conscience. Acknowledging your insecurities, coming to grips that you are not perfect (and do not have to be), you do not have to drive the biggest truck or suv, and openly admit that you have nothing to prove to nobody, not even God, you will find true happiness. God will judge you regardless if you are a good or bad person; and if you cannot figure this out, then no one can help you. Take a chance on yourself, be different, and stop falling in line like the rest of the universe, (stop being a human robot), not just a number; love yourself first. End the process of looking out your window to see what your neighbor has now, as (KJV)Ecclesiates 4;4 says; "And I saw that all labor and all achievement spring from man's envy having to go through some pain brings peace; the sky will not fall, I mean it will, but at least not tomorrow."

What wicked Gods we have; programming life like this on purpose, I keep telling you this, and you play right into their expectations, so easily. You were wired to crave attention, have insecurities, be a failure, and never be satisfied; and you were designed to be unimportant, lonely, miserable, and end up being happy. Less is more, and more is less. This is still an experiment and a game, and you have failed miserably. I cannot tell you what your future holds. I do not know my own future. But I ask of you; that you beat them at their own game.

We have lost our sense of self and humanity many, many, many years ago. In addition, with the technologies coming into play in the future, we will be worse off than better. I read an article that reported that the creators of these new technologies do not let their own children interact with the products until the age of 16-18, because it is so damaging to the mind, and body. Yet, your children are networking with computers, tablets, phones, at the youngest of ages, ruining them from the start. Congratulations on being a wonderful parent. Tech companies do not care about you, your children, or your family; all they see is dollar bill signs. These include the owners of gateway, dell, google, the good God says he can handle your curses, anger, backlash, and hate towards him, but I do not believe he can. However, I can, there will be many who will despise me for writing the truth; but it's okay, I still love you, and you have

It is already here!

already realized the certainty of this. In addition, I will not be the one sending you to hell, that's Jesus' job. I have proven that the good God Yahweh is in fact; not a loving, generous creator, but the opposite, masking as a warden.

I have noticed through the course of my life, that people make excuses for the good God and cover up for his mistakes even when they know he is wrong. If he is the supreme being, he should make no mistakes to begin with, right, he claims to be perfect. Moving on, they do this because there is no other option. We have to deal with an arrogant, detrimental, ruthless dictator as our creator. Your good God Yahweh is involved and has everything to do with evil in your life, never forget that; he just loves the fact that someone else take the blame for it; being the evil God Satan.

I love these guys, who I am about to mention. They have done more for humanity than your local billionaire has, but you have never heard of them. I will let the world know about them; if you want to know what your governments, hollywood, military, education systems are doing to you and your children directly, please research these tremendous people, this should get you started:

## Authors on books about the Illuminati
Jordan Maxwell, Michael Tsarion, David Livingstone,
David Icke, Mark Dice, Richard M. Dolan,
Dan Brown, Daniel Estulin, Brad Thor,
Kate Mosse, Julia Navarro, Jim Marrs

## Authors on books about the Government
Janet Ossebaard, Fritz Springmeier, Karl Marx,
Jesse Ventura, Suzanne Collins, John Rawls,
Bob Woodward, George Orwell, Michael Lewis,
Peter Dale Scott, David Wise, Thomas Paine,

**Authors on books about Hollywood**
Mark Manson, David McClintick, Elia Kazan,
Kieron Connolly, Michael Tolkin, David Rensin,

**Authors on books about the Galaxy, our Earth**
Santos Bonacci, Joseph P. Farrell, Mike Wall,
Ron Rosenbaum, Daniel Whiteson, Robert M. Hazen
Peter Ward, Joanna Martine Woolfold, Joe Kirschvink,
Elizabeth Tasker, Caleb Scharf, Chris Ferrie

# What is a false flag

A false flag is intentional misrepresentation, especially a covert political or military operation carried out to appear as if another party undertook it. The Sandy Hook Elementary School shooting occurred on December 14, 2012, in Newtown, Connecticut; and at Marjory Douglas High School, February 14, 2018, a gunman opened fire with a semi-automatic rifle in Parkland, Florida. False flags are a covert operation designed to deceive; the deception creates the appearance of a particular party, group, or nation being responsible for some activity, disguising the actual source of responsibility. The term "false flag" originally referred to pirate ships that flew flags of countries as a disguise to prevent their victims from fleeing or preparing for battle. Sometimes the flag would remain and the blame for the attack be laid incorrectly on another country. The term today extends beyond naval encounters to include countries that organize attacks on themselves and make the attacks appear to be by enemy nations or terrorists, thus giving the nation that was supposedly attacked a pretext for domestic repression and foreign military aggression.

Operations carried out during peacetime by civilian organizations, as well as covert government agencies, can (by extension) also be called false flag operations if they seek to hide the real organization behind an operation. You wonder how these people are able to acquire the types of weapons that they do: it is because they have former connections with the government and military and are brainwashed. It is the government's plan to remove your guns and enforce martial law in the united states of America. No one loves you except yourself, and if you do not love yourself, I cannot help you. USA or any government cannot have you knowing that they are behind these actions. Their desire is to control you, as they are doing now and you cannot even realize it. My soul is at peace. The government uses people that are mentally unstable and have nothing to live for to carry out these tasks; that way no one will miss them when they are gone. Yes, it is pretty sad if you ask me. When will you learn that no one cares for you? (QUR)-3 Family of Iran, v 26S says; "O God, Owner of Sovereignty. You grant sovereignty to whom you will, and You strip sovereignty from whom you will. You honor whom you will, and you humiliate whom you will. In Your hand is all goodness. You are Capable of all things."

It is amazing that, what you believe to be right, is wrong; and what is wrong is right.

# DAY 30: STAGE 30

God told me a long, long time ago that the world is not what it seems to be.

My heart is not cold, it is looking for a god to step up and do something to help, but no one is there. This is a cold, cold world, and you may or may not have never asked yourself this question or thought about it, but it is a legitimate question and comment. The meaning of life is to suffer and to be the god's-yes plural-god's, slaves. There, I gave it to you; you have been searching for it your entire life! There are three types of people in the world; number one has absolutely no idea of what is really going on; number two has an idea but does nothing about it; number three has a clue of what is going on and tries to make a change. This world is god Yahweh's prison for you. If you view something as a blessing, it is, but it is what he wants/never what you desire. Stop dreaming, wondering, and fantasizing: these things do not exist; and if they do, does not last. It is only given to you as a commodity for which you need in order to complete the experiment. God Yahweh tells you that you will be persecuted in your life: the one thing he does not tell you is that you are persecuted by him. You do not have to pretend that life is good anymore. Stop agreeing to a lie, false statements, and reaching for something that will never arrive. Commit mental suicide and jump off the bridge of what you are used to and find what your reality really is. Quit hiding your pain, your emotions, and your normal way of thinking because it has gotten you nowhere. The billionaire is just as sad and pathetic as a homeless person; the ceo is just as stressed out as the single mother; you believe you are found, you are a lost soul. You go to work every day like a slave, you think your money is yours but it is not, an earthly judge will be judged by god just like you.

Brokenness, heartache, sadness, agony, worry, battered, fear, anger and bruised are programmed emotions of a human being, yes, this is not a loving god because you experience those more than you experience love, joy, peace, goodness, faithfulness, patience, kindness, self-control, gentleness. My father has always pointed out that 'do I think I am the only one upset and angry with this type of life and situations'. No, I do not, but I am the only one willing to stand up to God and say you suck, this sucks, and maybe I would love you if you did things differently. Do not roll your eyes of what I just said because you act as if you know these things and you really do not. I have a voice, you have a voice, even in regard to god. Regardless of your race, color, religion and creed: you all try to act smart in front of your family, friends, coworkers and you have no idea of what is really going on. The government, nasa, others such as myself know this simple truth but the world lives with an attitude of what the world does not know, it will not hurt them. He sure had me fooled, but not for very long: fooled in the manner that the good almighty God ever cared, loved, and had an interest for me. I am not a hypocritical Christian; a back-biting Baptist; a deceptive catholic; a polygamist Mormon; a person looking for fame and fortune: just searched for the truth. The best thing that anyone could ever do is to die and the worst is being born. I, you have a huge enemy and we didn't even ask for him. He gives you want he wants; not want you need. You are not here to be rich; you are here to suffer. You are not here to be happy; you are here to be sad. You are not here to be good; you are here to be bad. God thinks he is so smart and you are so dumb that he has indirectly destroyed your lives by believing that he is good.

## **Thank you Almighty God Yahweh for having no discrimination in your evilness**

The almighty God creator has two sides: one of jealously and one of hate waning more on the side of hate. I want to thank the alleged good God Yahweh right now. I do not need to listen to false preachers/pastors and fake religious communities to figure out who God really is. They are confused-I know, they are only after your money and can care less where your soul is headed. They believe with all their hearts that the Almighty God is kind, generous, warm, and gentle. I have found that the simple nature of the general mass of inhabitants is okay with 'needing to believe in something good and discarding reality, and true information that is right in front of their faces'. The average religious person has not even read 1/2 of the bible, and if they did read the whole book, cannot understand what they are reading; but want to tell you what they know, how to live your life, and how to have faith. Thank you for the stress I never asked for, the hurt I never wanted, the bills I never requested, the death of a loved one I never needed, the domestic violence your sister is receiving, your kidnapped child that was murdered, your mother that was raped, your niece that is being sexually assaulted by your grandfather, the homeless person peeing and popping in the river, the woman who has arthritis in her knees from living in her car, for the police officer shooting an 18 year old about to start college, for believing in marriage but never helping them stay married, the bus of people that were blown up by a terrorist, the store that was shot up by a mental unstable person, the woman being harassed at work, the man without a job, and still looking, the child born with no arms or legs, the man bound to a wheelchair since birth, I thank you almighty God Yahweh, for showing who you really are.

This god Yahweh actually tells you to be joyful in your sufferings. (KJV)-James 1:1-7 says to you; "Consider it pure joy, my brothers, whenever you face trials of many kinds, because you know that the testing of your faith develops perseverance. Perseverance must finish its work so that you may be mature and complete, not lacking anything. If any of you lacks wisdom, he should ask god Yahweh, who gives generously to all without finding fault, and it will be given to him. But when he asks, he must believe and not doubt, because he who doubts is like a wave of the sea, blown and tossed by the wind. That man should not think he will receive anything from the lord." How evil is that, but this comes from your loving god. He wants you to fall, and crawl to him on hands and knees so he can, so call, save you from your sins: no my friend, it is to control you. The closer you are to wrong is the closer you are to right and the closer you are to right is the closer you are to wrong.

Now that you have the meaning of life: what will you do with it? This is a god who wants to control you and if you obey; heaven is promised: if you do not; hell is promised, what a sick, demented, domineering way of thinking. You are cursed either way. But every individual has the choice to make a judgment on their own accord: whether to be a good, kind, caring, and concerned person; or to be an evil, corrupt, hateful liar. Goodness and evil does not exist in our nature, only self-centeredness. Whether you decide to stop and help someone with a broken down car on the side of the road or not; is based on your self-centeredness. If you stop, you are stopping for your benefit; and if you do not stop, you are still doing it for your personal gain.

If you are willing to research, investigate, and find out the real truth: trust me, it is out there for you to learn. There is scripture telling us that Satan itself, is not a separate being, but actually a part of God; one of many faces of your so-called loving God. In all honesty, they are best friends, not enemies, and your life is just a gamble and wager between the two. There is no awesome, amazing God coming to save you from this current life of hell on this place we call earth, our home. Did you catch that? Your good and loving almighty God Yahweh is the one who creates evil, not God Satan; as Satan was the one you were led to believe since you were a child as evil. (KJV)-Isaiah 45:7; in the King James Version Bible, I say; "I form the light, and create darkness; I make peace, and I create evil; I the lord do all these things.", I, your creator, almighty God Yahweh does these things to you. You were not promised anything in this world, except to die at the end of your days.

Let me tell you about my last story of the evening. How many of you have worked for a moron, I mean a real moron. I worked for a person who owned a very small startup construction company in Eunice, LA. The point of this story is to reflect the stupidity and ignorance that comes out of people's mouths who believe they are something and are really nothing but dust waiting to be buried in the ground. He knows nothing about construction but one day I was reviewing architectural plans with him and an ambulance passes by the office with the sirens blaring. What comes out this persons mouth shows how stupid he is and the world because he is not the only one making these statements. He said as the vehicle passed, "I wish that they could be quieter in going to the accident." Now how pathetic is this? Paramedics were on their way to help someone who could possibly be dying or severely injured and if the shoe was on the other foot: I am one hundred percent confident that this person would want the ambulance to arrive as quickly as possible, at any and all costs but this is the kind of statements that are made when you believe you are a somebody and in actuality you are a nobody. I am pulling this out of the air, check my reference in (KJV)-Galatians 6:3-5 says to you; "For if anyone thinks he is something, when he is nothing, he deceives himself. Each one should test his own actions. Then he can take pride in himself, without comparing himself to somebody else, for each one should carry his own load." This particular person is not respected in the community, cheats on his wife-(amongst other items), is mean to his adult children, an angry, hateful being: and for what-money and reputation? You go to church but you make statements like this. It will be a cold day in hell before I affiliate myself with someone with this attitude.

## Who Really Knows Best?

See, I was cut from a different mold than you, your friends, and your family: the loneliness, uncertainty, pain, sadness, corruption, brokenness, misrepresentation and hate that I have felt during my time here is wrong and I refuse to hold my tongue. The bible/quran says that God Yahweh takes the worst people in the world and makes them good. Moses was a murderer, Paul was a violent man, Judas was jealous, Matthew was a corrupt, greedy tax collector; not because he wanted to, but because that is all he has to work with. I never became hooked on drugs, alcohol, a sexual addict, a greedy money ho-monger; this is the signs of a weak person with no self-identity. But yet my life has become a living hell, god does not care, why should I care about him? Why do I, you, have to keep waking up to the next day to nothing favorable, nothing positive, nothing new, nothing happy. I do not want heaven or hell, I just want to be left alone. I do not want to answer to anyone, anyone judging me, anyone loving me, anyone hating me, anyone consoling me, I just want to be left alone. Who goes through the daily trials and horror of life, you, not god. While God sits on his throne all nice, warm and comfortable; you struggle, you hurt, you cry, you worry, you hunger, you are in pain and you are depressed. Who knows best for you: god or yourself? You are in these situations, not him. When you make a decision, it is for your best interests: when he makes a decision, it is in his best interests; his will. I have seen this fight before and it cannot be won. These gods do not care or help anyone but themselves, how are they helping you when they take your job, letting you live in a car or on the streets, give you a divorce, your child dying, being raped, when you are exploited, when your body hurts; yeah, they are helping alright. God says he wants the best for you; but what does your reality say? He does not know what you experience down here on earth, just as you cannot experience what it is like to be a god. We live in two separate dimensions; he does not realize what you go through.

I will be the first and own up to, and take the responsibility for my emotions, affections, and fervor. I do not feel that god loves me. I do not feel that god cares for me. I do not feel that I matter; not in the world, but in god's eyes. I am happy because I choose to be happy. You are sad because you choose to be sad. If you would have been on 'the ship titanic' while it was going down in the Atlantic ocean; would you have fought for your life or just give into the sea for death. Some of you want to save the world and some want to destroy it; but it is not your yours to begin with. God wants you to call him lord and this simple fact says that he is the boss of you, needs to control you to be happy, inhibit you, and lie to you.

The God's ultimate plan was always to watch you; what you do, how you act, what you discover, what you invent, if you are nice or mean. Our world can be scary at times. With so much violence and uncertainty, we can feel vulnerable and confused. You are alone, God Yahweh always says The good that can come out of something bad isn't always obvious or immediate but that doesn't mean it's not there. If you continue to have difficulty having faith that God has His eyes on us, you can always call out to Him to help you recognize His presence. Sometimes we work hard to achieve a goal which benefits those around us, or put a lot of time and effort into overcoming a personal struggle but don't receive the recognition from our peers. It is not uncommon to feel unappreciated, devalued and almost invisible at times like this. However, God sees everything that we do and He rewards us for the good. We are not invisible to Him or without value. So much that there were a group of angels who eventually turned to demons whose specific job it was to watch everything you did and report to back to God Yahweh; they were called 'the watchers'.

I knew a man who served in world war II; became a very successful banker, acquired property, had a nice home and could afford anything he wanted; got married, had children and grandchildren: but at ninety-years old when he died in 2013, died alone in a one-bedroom apartment with no family or friends around. In saying farewell: you think you know things when you know absolutely nothing; your vision deceives you and your heart forsakes you; life fools you into believing you have something and you have nothing. My life, your life, is no different from this man. I exercise regularly to stay fit but at the same time I wonder why; why do this when my fate is death. You are one or two paychecks from living on the streets as well, so be nice to someone. The hate I feel from the gods lead me to conceive this book and release the truth; not my hate for the gods. I challenge you to see the evilness of your almighty creator Yahweh/Jehovah/ Allah/Abba/Adonai/El Elyon/El Olam/El Roi/El Shaddai. Money, fame, men, women, children, a job will never erase the pain you feel. The gods do not give you what you need; it is the opposite. (KJV)-Romans 11:32 the good god Yahweh; "has bound everyone over to disobedience so that he may have mercy on them all." Them all meaning all of you who walk the earth. God Yahweh made you a terrible person and then condemns you for your actions. Your suffering, pain and hurt is part of a bullshit plan developed by the gods. God claims to love and protect you but stand in front of a bullet and see how well that goes.

See how evil Yahweh is from (KJV)-Psalm 46:10; "Be still and know that I am God.". This is not a source of encouragement. It is a call to all the nations of the world to cease fire and bow down to the Lord who is God. "Be still and know that I am God" is not a great devotional memory verse; rather, it is a severe warning. This verse in context, is a warning to all of the armies of nations who oppose God and his people. It is as if God is saying, "Be still! Stop!!! CEASE FIRE! Know that I am God. I will be exalted among the nations. I will be exalted in the earth." Who has pride now? In other words, "If you oppose me, I will crush you. This is a battle that you cannot win." You are a product of your environment; but yet you are not. I have seen a person with all the opportunity in the world and blow it and I have seen someone with the worst circumstances succeed. Why does god hate you; because you do not listen, do not follow instructions, do not behave, and only worry about yourself; they do not want you to be you.

You can love God if you want, you are the fool. He knew that we could never control our desires, urges, dreams, wants and needs and still gave it to us: and then wants to condemn you and I for it. The Bible says that God hates some people and that many people are born with evil hearts. (KJV)-Romans 9:13-15 says that God hated Esau before Esau was even born, because Esau had inherited Adam's hatred of God, and God was not pleased (in His mysterious decision) to elect Esau to salvation. Yahweh will have mercy on those he wills and no mercy on those he who does not will. (KJV)- Psalm 5:5 says; "The arrogant cannot stand in Your presence; You hate all who do wrong." Notice that is it not some abstract "sin" or "wickedness" that God hates in this verse; it is people whom He hates.

(KJV)-Psalm 139:21–22 tells us that we should join God in His holy hatred of these people: "Do I not hate those who hate You, O Lord …? I have nothing but hatred for them; I count them as my enemies." The New Testament says the same in Revelation 2:6. How are we to understand this? In some cases, hate simply means "love less." But this is simply a stupid idea. In (KJV)-Luke 14:26 we find Jesus saying that we must hate the members of our own families if we want to follow Him, while in the parallel passage in (KJV)-Matthew 10:37, Jesus says we must love them less than we love Him. That kind of "soft" explanation, however, won't work in the passages we cited above. God did not love Esau less than Jacob; He did not love Esau in any saving way at all. It is (KJV)-Psalm 139:21–22 that gives us an important perspective on this matter. To hate someone is to count him as an enemy and to treat him as an enemy. In the Bible, hatred is not an emotion primarily, but rather a covenant action. Those who treat God as an enemy will find God treating them the same way. Since they are His enemies, and He "hates" them, He will destroy them.

The "soft" and the "hard" senses of hatred can be put together this way: When the Bible speaks of God's loving someone, it means He has chosen to favor them; when it speaks of God's hating someone, it means He has chosen not to favor them. Thus, we are to favor Christ and not favor the members of our families. Thus, God favored Jacob and did not favor Esau. Thus, we favor God's friends and we do not favor God's enemies (KJV)-Psalm 139. Favoring is a choice, not an emotion. When family members attack the church, we must choose to side with Christ. When God favors us, it means He elects us; those He disfavors, He leaves to their own damnation. (QUR)-Livestock ch 32 says; "The life of this world is nothing but a game and distraction, but the home of the hereafter is better for those who are righteous. Do you not understand?" I cannot let myself be upset with humanity; they did not create themselves, nor ask for this world. Therefore, they are not responsible for themselves and to finish it off, did you know that god Yahweh owns you, knows every single hair that is on your head-(KJV)-Luke 12:7. The ones to blame, I still will not allow myself to become mad over them; are the Gods. This life is worth nothing. What are you doing with your life; are you succeeding or failing?

God Yahweh and God Satan are sick individuals whose evils know no bounds.

# APPENDIX A

## Why Is There So Many Translations of the Holy Bible Presenting the Exact Same Concepts?

What is the Bible? The bible is scripture dedicated by Christians, Catholics, Baptists, etc. Because everyone wants to leave their mark in the world is the reason why there is so many different translations. Everything, I repeat, everything is about money and profit. The companies who distribute the books to the world do not read them and understand them. The Bible was originally written using 11,280 Hebrew, Aramaic, and Greek words, but the typical English translation uses only around 6,000 words with 66 chapters. An important fact is that we often miss the full impact of familiar Bible verses because you don't fully comprehend what it is saying and because they have become so familiar! We think we know what a verse is saying because we have read it or heard it so many times. Many, many people claim a verse is coming from the bible and it never did. This is why I have told you were to find the verses I use to state my facts. The fact that, God's truth in not loving you, and actually, hating you. Seeing your reality, it is not too hard to notice that God hates you.

| AMP | The Amplified Bible; it is largely a revision of the American Standard Version of 1901. It is now produced jointly by Zondervan and The Lockman Foundation. Its first edition was published in 1965. |
| --- | --- |
| CEV | Contemporary English Version; was first produced by the British and Foreign Bible Society. It is now produced by the American Bible Society. Its first edition was published in 1991. |

GWT     God's Word Translation; It is produced by the God's Word to the Nations Society. Its first edition was published in 1995.

KJV     King James Version; was first published by the Church of England, well before the 1500 century. It is the one that brings the old age and new age together.

LB     Living Bible; it is largely a revision of the American Standard Version of 1901. It is now produced by Kenneth N. Taylor and its first edition was published in 1971.

Msg     The Message; produced by Eugene H. Peterson and its first edition was published in 1993.

NAB     New American Bible; is the Catholic Church bible translation. It was originally published in 1970 by the Confraternity of Christian Doctrine.

NASB     New American Standard Bible; is an English translation first published in 1963 by The Lockman Foundation.

NCV     New Century Version; is a revision of the International Children's Bible. It has been a stand-alone version and published in 1991. It is produced by Thomas Nelson, a subsidiary of News Corp.

| NIV | New International Version; is an English International Version first published in 1978 by Biblica, formerly the International Bible Society. It works from the oldest copies of reliable texts: including Hebrew, Aramiac, and Greek prints. |
|---|---|
| NJB | New Jerusalem Bible; produced by Darton, Longman, Todd, and Les Editions du Cerf and its first edition was published in 1985. |
| NRSV | New Revised Standard Version; is an English translation published in 1989 by the National Council of Churches. |
| PH | New Testament in Modern English; |
| GNB/TEV | Good News Bible/Today's English Version; was first published in 1976 By the American Bible Society. |
| CSB | Holman Christian Standard Bible; the oldest bible publisher in America. |
| CWB | Clear Word Bible; first published in 1992. |

## Extra Verses to Study = You be the judge if these are true or not.

God Yahweh hates sin; but sins himself = (KJV)-Genesis ch 2; v15-17. (KJV)-Genesis ch 4; v 8-16. (KJV)-Genesis ch 6; v 5-8. (KJV)-Genesis ch 11; v 1-9. (KJV)-ch 19; v 1-38. (KJV)-Genesis ch 22; v 1-20. (KJV)-Genesis ch 38; v 6-7.

God Yahweh; your slave master = (KJV)-Exodus ch 1; v 11-22. (KJV)-Exodus ch 6; v 1-12. (KJV)-Exodus ch 8, 9, 10, 11. (KJV)-Exodus ch 12; v 12. (KJV)-Exodus ch 20; v 1-26.

God Yahweh; needs your attention = (KJV)-Leviticus ch 1, 2, 3, 4, 5, 6, 7.

(KJV)-Leviticus ch 13, 14. (KJV)-Leviticus ch 18. (KJV)-Leviticus ch 19. (KJV)-Leviticus ch 20; v1-27. (KJV)-Leviticus ch 21. (KJV)-Leviticus ch 26; v 1-46.

God Yahweh does things by the numbers = (KJV)-Numbers ch 5. (KJV)-Numbers ch 10.

(KJV)-Numbers ch 11. (KJV)-Numbers ch 23; v 19. (KJV)-Numbers ch 24; v 1.

God Yahweh; why does a God need sacrifices and offerings = (KJV)-Deuteronomy ch 5. (KJV)-Deuteronomy ch 6. (KJV)-Deuteronomy ch 13. (KJV)-Deuteronomy ch 17. (KJV)-Deuteronomy ch 20. (KJV)-Deuteronomy ch 26. (KJV)-Deuteronomy ch 30.

God Yahweh punishes you to no extent = (KJV)-Joshua ch 2; v 9. (KJV)-Joshua ch 8.

God Yahweh plays with your life = (KJV)-Judges ch 2; v 18. (KJV)-Judges ch 3; v 8. (KJV)-Judges ch 4. (KJV)-Judges ch 6; v 24. (KJV)-Judges ch 8; v 23. (KJV)-Judges ch 10.

God Yahweh; do not put your trust in this entity, trust yourself = (KJV)-Ruth ch 1; v 16.

(KJV)-Ruth ch 4; v 14.

God Yahweh; your God = (KJV)-1 Samuel ch 1; v 20. (KJV)-1 Samuel ch 2; v 3. (KJV)-1 Samuel ch 2; v 12-36. (KJV)-1 Samuel ch 15.

God Yahweh = (KJV)-2 Samuel ch 6; v 21. (KJV)-2 Samuel ch 7; v 28.

God Yahweh = (KJV)-1 Kings ch 8; v 56. (KJV)-1 Kings ch 11; v 1-13.

God Yahweh = (KJV)-2 Kings ch 1; v 12. (KJV)-2 Kings ch19; v 34.

God Yahweh = (KJV)-1 Chronicles ch 6; v 49-punishement. (KJV)-1 Chronicles ch 10 v 1-7. (KJV)-1 Chronicles ch 16; v 26. (KJV)-1 Chronicles ch 28; v 9.

God Yahweh = (KJV)-2 Chronicles ch 7; v 14. (KJV)-2 Chronicles ch 14; v 11.

(KJV)-2 Chronicles ch 16; 9. (KJV)-2 Chronicles ch 19; v 7. (KJV)-2 Chronicles ch 29; v 10. (KJV)-2 Chronicles ch 30; v 9. (KJV)-2 Chronicles ch 32; v 8.

God Yahweh = (KJV)-Ezra ch 2; v 11. (KJV)-Ezra ch 6; v 12.

God Yahweh = (KJV)-Nehemiah ch 1; v 6. (KJV)-Nehemiah ch 4; v 4. (KJV)-Nehemiah ch 8; v 7.

God Yahweh = (KJV)-Esther ch 2. (KJV)-Esther ch 3. (KJV)-Esther ch 7. (KJV)-Esther ch 9.

God Yahweh; you are a personal slave to him = (KJV)-Job ch 1; v 21. (KJV)-Job ch 2; v 11-13. (KJV)-Job ch 3. (KJV)-Job ch 5; v 17. (KJV)-Job ch 7; v 1. (KJV)-Job ch 14. (KJV)-Job ch 31; v 4. (KJV)-Job ch 36. (KJV)-Job ch 38.

God Yahweh; a fake = (KJV)-Psalm ch 4. (KJV)-Psalm ch 7. (KJV)-Psalm ch 10. (KJV)-Psalm ch 22. (KJV)-Psalm ch 24. (KJV)-Psalm ch 31. (KJV)-Psalm ch 35. (KJV)-Psalm ch 36.

(KJV)-Psalm ch 38. (KJV)-Psalm ch 49. (KJV)-Psalm ch 53. (KJV)-Psalm ch 59. (KJV)-Psalm ch 68. (KJV)-Psalm ch 74. (KJV)-Psalm ch 79. (KJV)-Psalm ch 83. (KJV)-Psalm ch 85. (KJV)-Psalm ch 94. (KJV)-Psalm ch 135.

God Yahweh = (KJV)-Proverbs ch 1. (KJV)-Proverbs ch 6. (KJV)-Proverbs ch 10. (KJV)-Proverbs ch 11. (KJV)-Proverbs ch 12. (KJV)-Proverbs ch 15. (KJV)-Proverbs ch 18.

(KJV)-Proverbs ch 22. (KJV)-Proverbs ch 24.

God Yahweh = (KJV)-Matthew ch 5. (KJV)-Matthew ch 7. (KJV)-Matthew ch 10; v 29.

(KJV)-Matthew ch 15. (KJV)-Matthew ch 25.

God Yahweh = (KJV)-Luke ch 4; v 18. (KJV)-Luke ch 6. (KJV)-Luke ch 11. (KJV)-Luke ch12; v 32. (KJV)-Luke ch 19; v 10. (KJV)-Luke ch 22; v 20. (KJV)-Luke ch 23; v 43.

God Yahweh = (KJV)-John ch 4; v 23. (KJV)-John ch 16; v 33. (KJV)-John ch 19; v 11.

God Yahweh = (KJV)-Romans ch 1; v 18-32. (KJV)-Romans ch 8; v 28. (KJV)-Romans ch 9; v 25-29. (KJV)-Romans ch 11; 33.

God Yahweh = (KJV)-1 Corinthians ch 1; v 8. (KJV)-1 Corinthians ch 6; v 20. (KJV)-1 Corinthians ch 10; v 13.

God Yahweh = (KJV)-Galatians ch 4; v 1-7. (KJV)-Galatians ch 5; v 22-23.

God Yahweh = (KJV)-Ephesians ch 6; v 5-9.

God Yahweh = (KJV)-Philippians ch 3.

God Yahweh = (KJV)-1 Thessalonians ch 4. (KJV)-1 Thessalonians ch 5; v 24.

God Yahweh = (KJV)-2 Thessalonians ch 1; v 6.

God Yahweh = (KJV)-1 Timothy ch 2. (KJV)-1 Timothy ch 5.

God Yahweh = (KJV)-Hebrews ch 5; v 11-14. (KJV)-Hebrews ch 7; v 25.

God Yahweh = (KJV)-James ch 3. (KJV)-James ch 4; v 13-17. (KJV)-James ch 5.

God Yahweh = (KJV)-1 John ch 2; v 15-17.

God Yahweh = (KJV)-Revelation ch 2-3. (KJV)-Revelation ch 3; v 21. (KJV)-Revelation ch 6; v 14. (KJV)-Revelation ch 6; v 15-17. (KJV)-Revelation ch 12. (KJV)-Revelation ch 15-18.

(KJV)-Revelation ch 22.

# APPENDIX B

What is the Quran? The Quran, meaning 'the recitation', is the bible for Muslims in the Middle East and throughout the world. There is one version of the Quran with many translations. The Quran is meant to achieve peace, but so is the King James Version Bible. The term Islam derives from the three letter Arabic root; S L M which generates the words surrender, commitment and peace. Islam is a world view religion focused on belief in one God and commitment to his commandments. Faith means that you have faith in God, his angles, his books, his messengers, and the last day (judgement day). This book discusses the same angels of the King James Version. It even mentions Jesus Christ, so why do certain personnel say that it is not of God. So the confusion comes in the form of the impact of Muhammad. I believe that Muhammad plays a role of someone like the apostles; writing the Quran. Someone who was relayed messages to put down on paper. The society during the time of Muhammad was predominantly oral and this is the reason he chose to write everything down for future generations. Ramadan is the month in which the Quran was revealed for the first time.

## Extra Verses to Study = You be the judge if these are true or not.

1- 'The Opening': v 2/, v 4/, v 7/.
2- 'The Heifer': v 5-7/, v 10-15/, v 16-18/, v 26/, v 40/, v 50/, v 62-67, v 72/, v 83/, v 90/, v 96/, v 102-105/, v 113/, v 115-119/, v 124/, v 155/, v 178/, v 186-195/, v 205-213/, v 217-238/, v 276-286/.
3- 'Family of Imran': v 3/, v 7/, v 13/, v 22/, v 25/, v 27/, v 32/, v 45-50/, v 55/, v 74/, v 145-160/, v 175/, v 185-186/, v 195/.

4- 'Women': v 1/, v 5/, v 17-18/, v 32/, v 52/, v 129-136, v 171-175/.

5- 'The Table': v 1-God decrees whatever he wills/, v 2-god is severe in punishment/, v 12-18, v 45/, v 66/, v 72/, v 90/.

6- 'The Livestock': v 1/, v 17/, v 32-39/, v 60-65, v 160/.

7- 'The Elevations': v 4-5/, v 32/, v 62/, v 87/.

8- 'The Spoils': v 55/. 9-'Repentance': v 80/. 10-'Jonah'; v 37/.

11- 'The Hud': v 2/.

13- 'Thunder': v 2/. 15-'The Rock': v 23/, v 35/.

16- 'The Bee': v 21/, v 51/, v 61/, v 70/, v 88/.

17- 'The Night Journey': v 53/. 18-'The Cave': v 6/, v 37/, v 55/.

19- 'Mary': v 40/, v 64-67/, v 83/.

20- 'Ta-Ha': v 53/, v 74/. 21-'The Prophets': v 25/. 22-'The Pilgrimage': v 1-2/.

23- 'The Believers': v 7/, v 14/, v 30/, v 65/, v 68/, v 70/.

24- 'The Light': v 64/. 25-'The Criterion': v 1-77/. 32-'Prostration': v 7/.

34- 'Sheba': v 33/. 35-'Originator': v 18-23/. 37-'The Aligners': v 30/. 38-'Saad': v 5/. 39-'Throngs': v 19/. 40-'Forgiver': v 17/. 41-'Detailed': v 22/, v 49/.

42- 'Consultation': v 8/. 43-'Decorations': v 2/, v 9-13/.

45- 'Kneeling': v 26/, v 34/. 46-'The Dunes': v 3/.

47- 'Muhammad': v 12-15, v 23-31/, v 43/.

48- 'Victory': v 2/. 49-'The Chambers': v 3/. 50-QAF': v 3/, v 29/.

51- 'The Spreaders': v 56/. 52-'The Mount': v 7/. 53-'The Star': v 11/, v 26/, v 38/.

54- 'The Moon': v 19-26/, v 53/. 55-'The Compassionate': v 14/, 33/.

56- 'The Inevitalbe': v 6/, v 8-9/. 57-'Iron': v 2-4.

58- 'The Argument': 1-22/. 59-'The Mobilization': v 2/, v 4/, v 16/, v 20/.

60- 'The Woman Tested': v 10/. 61-'Column': v 4/. 62-'Friday': v 4/, v 8/.

63- 'The Hypocrites': v 1-11/. 64-'Gathering': v 2/, v 8/, v 18/.

65- 'Divorce': v 2/, v 8/. 66-'Prohibition': v 2/, v 5/, v 9/.

67- 'The Sovereignty: v 2/, v 4/, v 6-12/. 68-'The Pen': v 7/, v 37/.

69- 'The Reality': v 1-3/, v 18/. 70-'Ways of Ascent': v 10/, v 41/.

71- 'Noah': v 3-4/, v 13/, v 23/. 72-'The Jinn': v 6/, v 12/, v 21/, v 22/.

75- 'Resurrection': v 5/, v 11/. 76-'Man': v 1-9/. 78-'The Event': v 18-20/.

81- 'The Rolling': v 10/, v 29/. 82-'The Shattering': v 1-19/.

84- 'The Rupture': v1-25/. 86-'The Nightly Visitor': v 4/, v 10/.

88- 'The Overshelming': v 1-25/. 96-'Clot': v 1-19/. 99-'The Quake': v 1-8/. 100-'The Racers': v 6-8/. 102-'Abundance': v 1-2/.

# APPENDIX C

## List of the lost books of the bible

Mentioned in stage one, these books where taken out of the bible during the time when Jesus Christ walked the earth. If I were to discuss all the sick things that happens in these books, it would blow your mind, so I will let you discover them for yourself. The list is below of the books of Apocrypha and the books of Pseudepiprapha.

### Apocrypha:

1. = 1.0 First book of Esdras-the fall of Jerusalem and their return home.
2. = 1.1 Second book of Esdras-Ezra's visions of the end times.
3. = 2.0 Book of Tobit-story of a Jewish man deported to Nineveh, in what is now Iraq. Against Assyrian law, he gives executed Jews a proper burial.
4. = 3.0 Book of Judith-a Jewish widow who saves her city from attacking Assyrians by seducing the enemies general, and then cutting off his head.
5. = 4.0 Book of additions to Esther-this Greek version of Esther's story adds more than fifty references to God. The Hebrew version doesn't mention him at all.
6. = 5.0 Book of wisdom of Solomon-similar to proverbs, this collection of quotes is supposed to point people to righteous living.
7. = 6.0 Book of Ecclesiastes-the book of Sirach-features songs and wise advice.
8. = 7.0 First book of Baruch-Baruch claims to be Jeremiah's assistant.
9. = 7.1 Second book of Baruch-extension of the first book.

10. = 8.0 Letter of Jeremiah-writes to exiles in Babylon, warning to not worship idols.
11. = 9.0 Song of the three holy children-children who fell on hard times.
12. = 10.0 Book of Susanna-was wrongly accused of having an affair with priests who were lying. She was so beautiful that they wanted her so badly.
13. = 11.0 Bel and the Dragon-worshipping fake Gods.
14. = 12.0 The Prayer of Azariah or addition to Daniel
15. = 13.0 The Prayer of Manasseh-the most evil jewish king to ever live.
16. = 14.0 First book of Maccabees-jewish priest lead a revolt against Syrian occupiers.
17. = 15.0 Second book of Maccabees-the war of independence.
18. = 16.0 Third book of Maccabees-protecting jews from an Egyptian king.
19. = 17.0 Fourth book of Maccabees-executing jews who do not abandon their faith.

## Pseudepiprapha:

1. = 1.0 Book of epistle of Barnabas - describing Jesus's life, time, and death as the messiah on earth. Praying to God when in need.
2. = 2.0 First book of Clement to the Corinthians - trouble in the Church; killing off priests, deacons, clergymen, nuns, and the laity, etc.
3. = 2.1 Second book of Clement to the Corinthians - diverting religion from paganism.
4. = 3.0 Martyrdom of Polycarp to the Smyrnaeans - you have to suffer as Jesus Christ did.
5. = 4.0 Shepherd of Hermas – visions of a former slave.

6. = 5.0 Book of Enoch - the truth of angels fleeing to earth from heaven and taking human form to have sexual intercourse with women because they were so beautiful. Their children were giants – 9ft to 15ft tall.

7. = 6.0 Gospel of Judas – conversations between Jesus and Judas.

8. = 7.0 Gospel of Thomas - the apostle who doubted the most.

9. = 8.0 The Psalm of Solomon - show a clear awareness of the Roman conquest of Jerusalem.

10. = 9.0 The odes of Solomon – letters written about Solomon.

11. = 10.0 Testament of Twelve Patriarchs – testaments about the twelve tribes of Israel.

12. = 11.0 Second book of Baruch -

13. = 12.0 First book of Adam and Eve – story about the experiences of the first couple.

14. = 13.0 The acts of Phillip – Philip's journey.

15. = 14.0 The apocalypse of Peter – first visions of heaven and hell.

16. = 15.0 Gospel of the Nativity of Mary – Jesus's mother.

17. = 16.0 Gospel of Nicodemus – describing Jesus's power and ability to do magic, work miracles, and raise souls from the dead.

18. = 17.0 First gospel of the Savior's Infancy – the gospels of Thomas.

19. = 18.0 The History of Joseph the Carpenter – story of Mary's Husband.

20. = 19.0 Acts of Paul and Thecla – building the church.

21. = 20.0 The seven epistles of St. Ignatius – Paul's letters to the world.

22. = 21.0 Epistle of Polycarp to the Philippians – early letters to the church.

# APPENDIX D

## The Dead Sea Scrolls

Mentioned in stage one, the Dead Sea Scrolls are a collection of 800-900 documents, many containing ancient Biblical texts. They were written over a period of around 200 years, and were evidently placed in the caves to hide them from the advancing Roman army at the time of the First Jewish Revolt, and hence no later than 68 AD. Carbon dating puts the earliest of them at about 150 BC. They may have been written out by the scribes of an ancient community living at Qumran, near the caves where they were found. However, their origins are the subject of much scholarly debate, and there are many different theories. What is clear is that the authors were Jewish, and disapproved of the Jerusalem priesthood of the time. They are basically the old testament in the KJV bible, etc. Some of the Apocrypha and Pseudepiprapha books are located in the dead sea scrolls. They were discovered in 1947 by the Dead Sea. Between 1947 and 1956, fragments were dug and unearthed from twelve caves in the nearby area. These were probably hidden to avoid trouble. The almighty God Yahweh seems to always place the people that he supposedly loves in bad situations. They eventually came out to the world, but at that time, you could have your head cut off, be imprisoned, or burned alive for writing or reading the word of God. Times seem different, but they are not. The more things change, the more they stay the same.

# DOES GOD REALLY LOVE YOU

Which God do you worship; religion, rituals, cult, denomination, study of theology or beliefs do you have? Why do you participate in all these different items when there is only one creator? And God, I get it. If you do not want to love us, then do not love us. We do not want to force you to do anything you do not want to do. The age old question is does God really love you? The answer to this question is NO. I never intended to be the person that tells the world the truth. The truth, that this life we individually live is just a game, an experiment gone horribly wrong, and as human beings, we were never afforded the chance to say, NO, I never desired this.

You are about to read one of the most unbelievable bible verses you will ever hear; yet you experience it in your every day life. Coming from the (King James Version), and all other bible versions-the book of Ecclesiastes ch 3, v 18-19, King Solomon says; "I said to myself concerning the sons of men-(man), God has surely tested them in order for them to see that they are but beasts-(animals). For the fate of the sons of men and the fate of beasts-(animals)- is the same. As one dies, so dies the other; indeed, they all have the same breath and there is no advantage for man over beast-(animal), for all is vanity."

(KJV)-Ephesians ch 6, v 12 is one of the most mis-understood verses; "For we do not wrestle against flesh and blood, but against the rulers, authorities, and cosmic powers over this present darkness, and against the spiritual forces of evil in the heavenly realms." Your Gods-God Yahweh-the true creater and ruler that holds the power of all things resides in heaven and god satan-(lucifer)-the devil was thrown out, so he is not in heaven: how simple is this to see in this verse that you battle against God Yahweh-your creator and not god satan. Satan cannot do anything to you without Yahweh's permission. Everyone here on earth is hurting, and wasting away:

and who is really to blame for these cruel, useless and unjust punishments? You may act as if you are better off than the next person, but you are not: I know better. You never create something that you cannot control, and Yahweh cannot control you. This is the spiritual being that claims to love you, but the physical world and your reality tell a very, very different story. Just because you can create something; does not mean that you should- the Gods do not want you to be happy. All of your internal questions are answered truthfully here. This is not another fairytale christian book not giving you the correct reply. They sit on the shelf year in and year out, but not this particular book.

Printed in the United States
by Baker & Taylor Publisher Services